MOSAIC MOON

CAREGIVING THROUGH POETRY

Dear Wendy,

You are truly a
winner... you wear
this on your face.

Frances H Kaleyuer
4/27/14

*This book is dedicated to our loved ones,
who taught us about love, dignity and honor
and who helped us to grow and to know life
beyond human suffering.*

Watermark Publishing
1088 Bishop Street, Suite 310
Honolulu, Hawaii 96813
Telephone: Toll-free 1-866-900-BOOK
Web site: www.bookshawaii.net
e-mail: sales@bookshawaii.net

ISBN 978-0-9720932-0-0 (softcover edition)
ISBN 978-1-9356900-4-7 (Kindle edition)
ISBN 978-1-9356900-5-4 (EPUB edition)

Library of Congress Control Number:
2002107301

Design and production by
Gonzalez Design Co.

All photographs by Ryan Hirasuna or from
contributors' collections except the following:
Eric Dinyer/Graphistock (cover)
Jason Kimura (ii-iii, xiv, 22, 102, 122,
    160, 178, 190)
Leo Gonzalez (104 bottom, 162 bottom,
    192 bottom, 199)
Cory Lum/*The Honolulu Advertiser* (193)

Printed in the United States of America

Contents

Acknowledgments

Mosaic Moon is a collaborative effort by many people, who came with heart and soul beyond words. Yet I find myself using these very words which limit me in attempting to express my gratitude to:

George Engebretson and Duane Kurisu of Watermark Publishing, for their faith and belief in our work and for making our dreams possible. A special thank you to George for taking this book beyond what it was at the beginning, a mere collection of poems.

Jason Kimura, editor of *Kakoʻo,* the newsletter of the Alzheimer's Association Aloha Chapter, for his portraits of our poets, for the biographical stories in this book, and for the elegant literary images brought forth from his journals at each of our sessions, revealing the splendor of his art and his soul.

Ryan Hirasuna, photographer and Boston College student. A former third-grade student of mine, Ryan said in class on numerous occasions, "When I grow up, I'm going to find a cure for Alzheimer's disease." His photographs — contributed in memory of his grandfather, George Hasegawa, who had AD — reflect his wisdom and understanding of our plight. At age 20, Ryan has surpassed me and become my teacher.

Ted Plaister, retired professor of English as a Second Language, for serving as my first editor with his wisecracking editorial pen, and for not accepting any postage reimbursement for all the mail between Hawai'i and California.

Caregivers Irene Asato, Lynne Halevi, Joyce Lani Kaaihue, Jody Mishan and Setsuko Yoshida, whose poems appear in this book. They were the courageous ones who came every month, fighting with everything humanly possible to rise above the effects of this devastating disease. Each of their triumphs can be seen in their poems.

Janet Bender, President and CEO of the Alzheimer's Association Aloha Chapter, for not needing any words to know why we are here. She has been the holder of the moon, encompassing each of us in the circle of her arms. There are no words to express my appreciation of who she is: caregiver, dream maker, friend.

Frances H. Kakugawa
Honolulu, Hawai'i

Foreword

Mosaic Moon – Caregiving Through Poetry grew from the experiences of caregivers who attend a special Poetry and Journaling Group, a workshop created by the Alzheimer's Association Aloha Chapter in Honolulu, Hawai'i. It is the wish of these caregivers that it serve as a blueprint for stepping outside the "burdens of care" and finding not only humor, but a path to inner peace in the process.

This is a source book of practices, beliefs, laughter and tears – a telling of families breaking apart and a telling of families coming together in renewed spirit, love and friendship. It is a document of how caregivers strive to create a balance of dignity and respect for their loved ones, while witnessing the loss of personhood caused by Alzheimer's. It is a testimony of loss and grieving, and of renewal and strength.

The objectives of this work are to provide through poetry a glimpse into the inner lives of caregivers, their rollercoaster day-to-day experiences, and solutions discovered along the journey through the disease process; to provide encouragement and a practical how-to work plan for those who want to document their experiences and create poetry but have never written in their lives; and to provide a testament to the very real lives and dignity of once vibrant, creative, successful human beings now robbed by a terrible disease.

Families and caregivers of loved ones with Alzheimer's disease often live in isolation from the rest of the world. It is difficult to explain to those outside the immediate family the events that present their daily trial. While there are many services and programs offered by the Alzheimer's Association, the challenge becomes one of assisting those who traditionally do not reach outside the family circle for support and guidance. It was from this perspective that the Alzheimer's Association's Poetry and Journaling Group was formed.

We are fortunate that Frances H. Kakugawa – a teacher, writer, published poet and caregiver for her beloved mother – agreed to be our *sensei* (respected teacher). Her belief in our wish to help other caregivers, and her insistence in including caregivers who had never written in the process, was of great value. Frances encouraged the participants in the group to report with raw honesty so that others may learn – to openly share their experiences, but always to honor the dignity of the loved one with Alzheimer's. Without her tenacity, passion and commitment, this work could not have been done.

I have personally watched this group of diverse individuals come together, most without any writing experience, as they evolved into poets, historians, diplomats, mediators and champions of their loved ones. I have watched them come together for each other, to laugh with each other, to grieve with each other, to stand by each other when a loved one passed away from the disease.

These were individuals who revealed from the start that they were not interested in attending a support group, but were drawn to the creative process of what we were starting at the Alzheimer's Association Aloha Chapter. In time, they became friends and fellow poets, creating a network of compassion, safety and strength for one another.

And finally, on a personal note: Thank you, Frances, for your courage, your honesty, your willingness to extend yourself to reach others while struggling through the process with your mother. Your courage to honor your mother by serving as her champion is a tribute to the woman who raised you. Thank you for trusting me when I coerced you into teaching others to join the ranks of poets. And thank you for your courage to become my friend.

To the readers of this book, my hope is that you will use it as a guide to create your own collection of poems, and that you will discover for yourself the words to release the deepest sharing of your experiences. Whether you are a caregiver for a person with Alzheimer's disease or a related dementia, or a caregiver for a loved one with any chronic devastating disease, we hope that you will find in these pages comfort and a means to embark on a path to transcend the burdens of care throughout your journey.

Janet Bender
President and CEO
Alzheimer's Association Aloha Chapter

Introduction

Mosaic Moon is more than a collection of poetry and photographic images reflecting the human experience of caring for victims of Alzheimer's Disease. It is meant as a resource guide – a hands-on tool designed to help caregivers and others explore and share that experience through creative expression. Its "how-to" approach to the writing process can be used by any organization planning poetry workshops, by informal support groups or simply by individuals working on their own. Although written by caregivers for caregivers, this book is for anyone who knows what it is to be human, and who wishes to transform that humanity into poetic form.

For more than a year, the caregivers and I, whose poems appear in these pages, met once a month in an attempt to make sense of this disease, to rise above the burden of care it imposes and to recapture the human spirit which is sometimes lost in day-to-day caregiving. This is our story.

We came from diverse backgrounds reflecting great differences in many areas. Our educational accomplishments ranged from high school diplomas to doctoral degrees. Our religions included the Jewish, Buddhist, Catholic and Protestant faiths. Racially and culturally, we represented Jewish, Japanese, Hawaiian, Russian, Hungarian, German and Polish roots. Our ages spanned 30 years.

Yet despite our differences, we transcended diversity and quickly came together as one, bonded both physically and spiritually by our need to survive the rigors of caring for loved ones with Alzheimer's disease. We sought each other out of need and in the end, it was from ourselves that we drew our greatest strength.

Our loved ones came from worlds as diverse as our own. Their educational backgrounds ranged from a fifth-grade education to Ph.D.s. Their varied cultural and racial heritages, their religious affiliations, their social and economic backgrounds were as varied as those of their caregivers. Alzheimer's disease, of course, practices no discrimination in those it chooses to afflict.

This journey was one of courage, as each of us faced the unknown with her own fears, feelings of helplessness, despair, pure exhaustion, hope, revelation and even humor – as the poems in these pages attest.

But relentless as the Alzheimer's thief may be, we were equally relentless in seeking what we call the *divine* in caregiving, just as the afflicted have been relentless in retaining their own human dignity. In our ongoing journey, one factor emerged: that victim and survivor, patient and caregiver, were often one and the same. Together we fought to live with human dignity and compassionate love, even as we lost many parts of ourselves in the progression of this disease. Both patients and caregivers slowly evolved into new people who simply hadn't existed before.

As our loved ones slowly diminished, we caregivers gradually grew into stronger, more compassionate, more humanistic beings. Our journey shows transformation in both our writings and in ourselves. This journey did not come easily, as these poems will reveal. Almost every caregiver's journey began with anger, frustration and confused helplessness. But with each session, negative attitudes and feelings began to dissipate, replaced by the renewal of a truer self.

One message was clear throughout our journey, which continues to this day: that only in darkness can a light be seen. Only in sunlight does a mosaic moon reveal its full glory.

Mosaic Moon

Frances H. Kakugawa

My mosaic moon comes to life
Through the rays of the sunlight.
How deceiving to my eyes
When it first appears as one
Like that moon full in the night.
At closer look, my moon is one
Of varied shapes and pieces
Carefully shaped, formed, fitted,
Held together by some mysterious hand.

> Lynne, child of the moon,
> Whose poems, drenched in tears
> Speak of lost love, yet unashamed,
> She courageously sought companionship
> In her Victor of long ago, at concerts,
> movies and operas
> Until death did them part.
> Lani, youngster of the moon,
> Whose wisdom surpasses the aged.
> Sharp as a sword, soft as the morning mist
> Her metaphors bring solace,
> Her internal cue cards, laughter breaks
> When most needed.
> Sets, the spiritual child
> Who seeks the divine tenaciously.

Her relentless pursuit weakens the thief
Who has stolen her Patrick
So many times over and now forever.
Irene, God's child
Whose newly discovered love for her mother
Brings knowledge and acceptance,
Gratitude and peace
To her once hours of despair,
Accompanied now by her spiritual Being.
Jody, the strong, the learned, the dancer
Whose dance has altered to an unknown beat.
Love for her father creates a new self,
Unchartered, undefined, unsolicited.
Her trials and tribulations rip into her
Like tornadoes on a quiet afternoon.
My mosaic moon rises
Once a month,
Radiantly aglow
With each ray of the sun.

Phases of Mosaic Moon

How do you learn to write poetry when you're not a poet? How do we express ourselves in poetic form when we may not be comfortable expressing ourselves on paper at all? At our caregivers poetry workshops, held in a meeting room at our local Alzheimer's Association chapter, we explored this process over a period of many months. What follows is a kind of road map of that journey. You can use it as a guide to starting a similar program in an organized group, or simply follow along on your own.

There are many different avenues to creative expression, of course. What you'll find here is simply my own personal approach to helping others write poetry. This section will guide you through the same process that our group members followed. They, too, approached poetry with a tentative "How do I begin? Where do I start?" The techniques offered here are for beginning writers. At the end of this section, you'll find a suggested list of resource books that can help, along with a summary of some basic steps to writing poetry.

Because keeping a journal is a key part of the process, this section is presented within the framework of my own journal – entries that recorded exactly what the caregivers and I went through every step of the way.

My suggestion is to first enjoy the poems in this book, then return to this section and use it as your own personal writing workshop, creating along with our caregivers. When they are asked to write a journal entry, for instance, you can write one yourself. Again, this can be done individually or in a group.

So come, gently walk and stumble along with us…

May 27

Well, I arrogantly walked unannounced into the office of Janet Bender, President and CEO of the Alzheimer's Association Aloha Chapter, introduced myself and showed her some of the poems I've written on being a caregiver for my mother. When I saw her tears and felt her hug, I felt so connected at a very poetic level that I knew I was in the right place.

January 19

It's a very good thing Janet doesn't throw out unannounced visitors, because once again I walked in without an appointment and volunteered to do a poetry workshop for caregivers to help them cope with the tremendous burden of caring for an Alzheimer's patient. I truly believe I can help others transcend the burden of care to that of the divine through writing. Janet knew why I was there even before I had made my offer and she suggested an article in *Kako'o*, the monthly newsletter of the Alzheimer's Association Aloha Chapter.

February 5

Jason Kimura, editor of the newsletter, came to interview me for the story. I was pleasantly surprised how my mother sat and crocheted for two hours during our interview, occasionally looking at me for assurance that I was still there with her. I also interviewed Jason and learned of his passion for writing.

March 5

A lead article titled "Transcending the Burden of Care" with my photo appeared in this month's newsletter with the story of how I was using poetry writing as a means of seeking the divine in caregiving. The date of our first workshop along with three of my poems were also included. Jason has a good camera. It eliminates facial wrinkles very well.

March 10

How will tomorrow's first session go? I bribed my

friend Cathy, whose mother has Alzheimer's, to attend because "it would be so embarrassing if no one showed up." I promised to buy Cathy lunch.

I can already see us a year from now, doing poetry readings from our own published book. I truly believe there is in all of us, a poet and all one needs is a bit of nudging to get this poet out.

March 11

I took a vase of roses and lighted a red candle so our setting was poetically calming.

Twelve people quietly filled the room, including two men. Except for Jason, they all said they haven't written anything before, but they want to find the divine like me and if they can discover it through writing, they're game.

To set the tone, and to take them directly into the reason why we were there, I began by reading some of my own poems about caregiving. I felt that experiencing poetry firsthand would make more of an impact than just talking about it. Two boxes of Kleenex were passed around. One woman held on to another as they wept. I also read a few of my journal entries to give them some idea of journal writing. They nodded to my comment that journal writing is very private and we share these entries only if we so wish.

I suggested we all try some writing. "Do not try to overwhelm yourself with too big a picture," I cautioned them. "Instead of writing about a forest, write about a single tree or a blade of grass. Instead of trying to write about the overwhelming role of caregiving, write about one aspect. What are you feeling right now? Reach down deep into yourself at the gut level and begin there."

They all began writing, a few repeating loudly, "One blade of grass, not the whole forest."

After 20 minutes of writing we stopped and a few shared their entries. Irene began to read and stopped because of her tears. Her entry spoke of her mother being ill for ten years, her past negative relationship with her and of the love she now feels. She looked surprised; until this moment, she said, she'd been stuck on the old relationship. "You have found a part of the divine that you came to find," I told her, and she said, "Yes." Sharing our writing was already drawing us closer within the caregivers' common circle of pain.

Sets, meanwhile, verbally expressed her negative feelings and tried to apologize that she couldn't be like me. I suggested that she begin with those negative feelings. This is her entry:

> Poems read by Frances Kakugawa this morning reveal the feelings of "Divine" in caregiving. How can this be? How do I reach this point in caring for my 84-year-old husband who is returning to childlike ways? I have such anger, resentment and frustrations at times that overwhelm me at unexpected moments throughout the days and nights. How do I deal with my negative thoughts and feelings? Could poetry and journal writing bring me some solace to truly see me for who I am?

After she shared that entry with us, I read a journal entry of my own dated February 10:

> Sometimes when I walk into the Adult Care Center and see the men and women sitting, looking at nothing from where I stand, I can't help but wonder if there is a loving God. If there is, why hasn't He taken all these people home instead of letting them live this way. Then another part of me says, "Maybe they are all here for a purpose...to help us, their caregivers, discover what compassion and love are all about. Maybe after He is through with us, He will take them all home. I still recall Michener's line in his last novel Centennial, that if you want to see what love is all about, observe a caregiver with an Alzheimer's patient. Maybe I have not reached that depth of pure love yet.

Then, to show how we can sometimes lift a poem right out of our journal, I read the poem I had written from that entry:

Before the Journey Home

I walk into the day care center
And am greeted by men and women
Staring at nothing from where I can see.

If there is a loving God
Why hasn't He taken all of you home
When living has put you in wheelchairs
Without speech or memory?

You sit here day after day
Waiting, waiting, for what or for whom
I do not know.
You look past me so I know
It is not I for whom you wait.

My mother's face greets me
Among all the silent faces.
Oh, perhaps you are here for us,
The healthy and the strong,
To help us discover what love
And compassion are all about.

Perhaps, after He has done
His work with us,
He will take you all home.

I explained how poetry can say, with the least number of words, what you want to express. Look for that one blade of grass and focus on that. I did it in the poem above with one idea – that perhaps these men and women are not ready to be taken "home" because He is not through with us as caregivers, as compassionate human beings of the purest form.

Then I lightly touched on the writing process itself, using the following diagram:

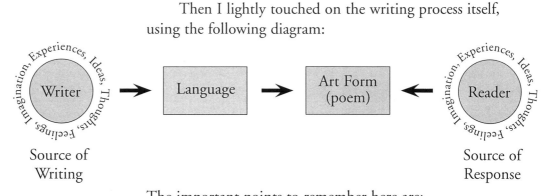

The important points to remember here are:

- A writer's source of inspiration is his or her own experiences, ideas, feelings, thoughts and imagination.

- The only tool available to express these resources into writing is language.

- With this language, writers are able to communicate their human experiences and emotions into an art form such as, in this case, a poem.

- This poem is then read by others who use their own human experiences, feelings, ideas, thoughts and imagination to derive meaning from the art form.

I showed the group a dictionary and said, "All the words found in a Nobel Prize-winning anthology or a Pulitzer Prize-winning novel are found in this dictionary. It's how we use these words that makes for successful writing."

We often need to create images beyond what our senses have seen, heard, touched, felt or smelled. I shared the following:

I was stuck in traffic with my mother at my side. We sat in the car near an overpass. I watched this woman walk across the overpass, carrying a black umbrella. I sat there and thought, "Now if that woman had a red umbrella, it would create a lovelier image. Red against that blue sky. Better yet, if a child was walking with that umbrella, I would see only the umbrella walking."

That night I wrote the following poem about that morning's experience. I asked them to note the poetic license I took in recreating some of the images to empower my poem.

A Red Umbrella

A red umbrella

Moves across the overpass

I smile as I sit

In traffic below.

Is it a child

Late for school

Or did Mary Poppins

Get lost in flight?

Such frivolous thoughts

As I drive my mother

To Adult Day Care.

Once again, I explained how I had sought that one blade of grass. There were high-rise buildings, traffic all around me, my mother in the car, the woman on the overpass. But I chose that one moving umbrella as my focal point. I also took poetic license and changed the color and the person carrying the umbrella to create a more distinct image.

I suggested that they all continue writing at home. If they wished to send me their journal entries, I would help lift their poems out. I gave them my mailing and e-mail addresses. We ended the session sharing stories of some of the common problems we were encountering in caregiving.

April 8

Only six of us attended our second session today. I had called Sets a week ago and helped her lift the following poem from her last journal entry which she now proudly shared:

Can I?

Sets Yoshida

Poems by Frances this morning
Reveal the feelings of "divine"
In caregiving.

How can this be?
Can I, too, reach this point
In caring for my 84-year-old husband
Who is returning to childlike ways?

Anger, resentment and frustrations
Overwhelm me at unexpected moments
Throughout the days and nights.

How can I deal with such thoughts and feelings?
Can poetry and journal writing bring me some solace
To truly see me for who I am?

I pointed out how I did not change any of Sets' words except to drop a few words and rearrange her narrative form into poetic lines. She had the poem buried in narrative form. Where needed, I suggested they use the present tense to bring a sense of reality, that sense of having it happen right now instead of being a thing of the past, thus weakening the impact.

Sharing the journal entries along with the poems have helped a lot as most of the participants came with poems. A few chose to sit and listen.

The group decided to meet once a month.

May 6

There were thirteen of us today at our third session. The article "A Journey to the Divine Continues," featuring Sets in the May issue of our newsletter, helped confirm my belief that we are able to rise above the burden of care through writing – just as Sets was experiencing personally.

The caregivers are coming to the sessions with poems all written and ready to share, accompanied by a lot of tears and stories to tell. Hearing poems written by others gives us permission to be honest. Having copies of our poems in everyone's hands can become a model for others, as we see and share these concrete forms and uses of language.

July 8

Lynne said something so powerful today: "I've been to other support groups and they do a lot of bleeding without coagulating. This one does."

November 4

Sets' husband, Patrick, died last month. Our session was solemn and yet so comforting. We sat more in silence than in talk. Silence and sadness are good. I tried to maintain this mood, wanting everyone to be comfortable, for we need to flow naturally with these moments and see where they will take us. We continued to write.

December 9

Even Steven Spielberg couldn't have scripted a better session. Today I walked out feeling that the group members are doing well on their own and that my presence is no longer needed. What a place to come to in just nine months!

Sets read a letter she had written to us about Patrick's death, crediting me as her mentor, spiritual friend and leader, and thanking the group for the support she has received. Everyone wept openly.

Lynne shared how, in the middle of cleaning up the results of her husband's incontinence, she saw the image of me in my feather boa described in my poem *A Feather Boa and a Toothbrush* (page 37), and how she'd heard me saying, "It's okay; clean this up and you can write about this." She wept and wept as she read her poem.

That's very humbling – to think my voice is being heard in the midst of incontinence.

The tears, laughter and teasing, as well as a spiritual bonding that was truly magical in nature, moved me to write the following poem:

A silk thread,

A string,

A rope,

A cable.

Finally, nothing

Visible to the eyes.

Bonded for life

Soul to soul,

The human spirit.

January 6

I read the following poem written after our last session to show how far we have come:

She was the first to drop her armor
At the round table that spring morn.
"I am here," she announced,

> "Because I am angry,
>
> Frustrated, exhausted.

The First Nightfall

> Can I reach the divine as you?"

She pointedly said to me,
Challenging me to make true my words
That we are all capable of rising above the burden of care
Through the ink that flows from deep within.

We had come to a place,
A place without commitment,
A place without expectations,
A place without failures,
Yet each sat at the edge, unsettled, uncertain,
Questioning not only the opposing forces
Of Alzheimer's but my voice that spoke
Like some mysterious ally of the foe.

She was the first to lay down her shield,
The first to place her fingers around her pen.
She pursued her quest, exploring every inch of her battle
From depths where feelings and attitudes
Gave way to her spiritual freedom.
And soon, the others who had come,
Began to drop their armor

And as they felt the sting and pain
Of each dart and arrow piercing
Through their vulnerable selves,

The stronger they became.
Fear, helplessness, grief, confusion
Emerged into poetry of their soul,
Turning each toward the divine.

Today she was once again the first,
The first to lose a loved one to the foe.
We met once again around the table,
A table without edges, poetry without words,
Their armors long gone, tears spent.
We met to honor the valiant, the courageous, the broken
In both victim and survivor.
The spiritual link around the table held us as one,
As we silently acknowledged the presence of God
Who had nurtured, loved, prepared us
For the passing of another night.

January 7

An article appeared in our morning paper, *The Honolulu Advertiser*, featuring the work I was doing with the Alzheimer's Association through this journaling and poetry group. This resulted in many telephone calls and a few new members. One caller said, "My wife and I want to feel this joy, too," referring to *Joy*, one of my poems quoted in the paper (page 44).

February 10

By now, of course, we are all comfortable with each other and with our own writing, which helps a great deal in the sharing process. Having a copy of others' poems in our hands helps us each move to higher levels of writing, as we use their poems as models for discussion. Our group members are also reading other published poems.

Today I handed out a list of literary devices, culled from a middle-school English textbook, that can be incorporated into our writing. (The fact is, many of our group members are already using many of these devices.) Because our workshop members are still beginning writers, I've introduced only very basic literary devices and techniques. For example, we use free verse instead of any of the traditional forms requiring certain rhyme schemes and meter. For those interested in exploring more advanced language devices and poetic forms, I suggested a few good resource books (listed at the end of this section).

Following are some the basic devices and techniques, illustrated by examples from the caregivers' poems in this book.

Imagery

The images language creates in our senses. The more detailed and descriptive the image, the better the images. We explored visual imagery with exercises like:

Can your use of language create images in a person's mind? Close your eyes. I'm going to describe a flower. What do you see if I say, "A beautiful flower"? (Many described various flowers.) How about "A red rose lifts her velvet face toward the sun"? (All described a red rose.) Which gives you a clearer image, closer to what I'm describing?

Simile

Two objects or entities are compared, using like or as. In the poem *My Pet Father* on page 213, Jody compares herself to a beast of burden, given all the physical work she's required to do:

"and carry the bags in, feeling like a pack mule."

Note how this comparison gives us a clearer idea of how she really feels. We can appreciate the burden on her back, like a pack mule struggling under a heavy load. The line creates strong imagery, much better than simply, "I'm tired."

Or consider the poem *Drinking the Sea* (page 140) in which Lani makes the following comparison to describe the almost impossible life of a caregiver.

"Being a caregiver is like drinking the sea."

Metaphor

Unlike similes, words "like" and "as" are not used in metaphors. Instead we say that one thing is the other. In many of my poems, for instance, I use "thief" to describe Alzheimer's disease. And in the poem *Family Dynamics* on page 92 I use a couple of metaphors to describe how this disease can destroy families just as an earthquake can destroy a house. Here the earthquake is the disease, while heirlooms are our family relationships:

uncontrollable rocking, crescendoing into destruction...
dislodging family heirlooms, soon shattered on floors...

Symbol

A concrete or real object used to represent an idea. Wings, for example, are often used as a symbol of freedom. In my poem *Wings* on page 68, butterfly wings are used as a symbol of freedom.

...freedom comes not with wings...

Allusions

A reference is made to a well-known person, place, thing or event that is assumed to be familiar to the reader. In my poem *Rilke's Panther* on page 52, I allude to the poet Rainer Maria Rilke's poem *The Panther* and describe a person with Alzheimer's being caged like that panther. (Note that a simile is also used here.)

"Like Rilke's Panther they live behind bars."

Or in *Mr. Thief* on page 87 I use an allusion to the escape artist Harry Houdini, observing how Alzheimer's disease eludes a cure just like one of Houdini's baffling tricks. Just one word, like "Houdini," can express a complex idea without any explanation. Many of us know the children's book figure Waldo from the *Where's Waldo?* series. Lani alludes to him in *Where's Hideko?* on page 140.

> *"Where's Waldo?" is like her mother's life now"...*

The allusion here suggests the difficulty her mother is encountering in finding who she's looking for.

Alliteration

Words with similar consonants sounds at the beginning of words are repeated in a line or lines. In the poem *Fall*, I use words with the successive beginning consonants "s" and "b".

> *In the midst of sadness and sorrow,*
> *I had sought beauty, beauty created*
> *By the last breath of summer.*

In the poem *Chop Suey Saturday* on page 171, Sets also uses the "s" sound:

> *Stroking Tiger, our striped male cat*
> *Sleeping soundly beside him...*

March 10

The group has playfully labeled me "General," from Lani's poem *Siege Warriors* on page 127. So taking advantage of this, I am freely giving "commands" to a group of obedient warriors. On revisions, for instance:

- The best way to check rhythm, tone and sound at this beginning level is to read your poems aloud. This leads to editing where we look for another word or words or rearrange lines to smooth out the rhythm and sound of the poem.

- Writers constantly reread and revise their work. Poems are not born overnight. Like poets, they evolve with time and pain. Some of my poems took over six months before I could say, "Done, I think." You may want to return to some of your poems and include a few language devices. And remember, you are the final decision maker.

Below is a first draft of my poem *A Feather Boa and a Toothbrush,* including all the revisions. I went through more than six sittings to get to the final copy. The last two lines were changed nine months later, after I received feedback from our writing support group. The final version appears on page 37.

A Feather Boa and a Toothbrush

It is
~~It's~~ 3 a.m.
I am ~~I'm~~ on my hands + knees ~~off~~   BM?
Scrubbing ~~doo-doo~~   Incontinence?
                                                        feces?
My mother's bathroom ^floor
With ~~a~~ toothbrush in one hand
And a ~~glass~~ cup of hot tap water in my ~~m~~ other.

Before a flicker of self pity can set in,
        vivid
An ^ image enters my mind,
An image Of a scarlet feather boa
        Impulsively bought from Neiman Marcus,
^ wrapped ~~delicately~~ in white tissue ~~paper~~
Awaiting in my cedar chest
                enchanting enchanted
For some special evening.
The contrast between my illusional lifestyle
                        opium
Of feather boas, ^ perfume + black velvet
And my own reality of scrubbing
~~Doo-doo~~ at 3 a.m.   silent
Overwhelms me with ^ laughter.

Of toothbrushes, bathroom tiles and BM
Overwhelms me with silent laughter.
Of toothbrushes, bathroom tiles and B.M. at 3 a.m.
* Overwhelms me with silent laughter.

We celebrated our one-year anniversary with chocolates and chardonnay. I read the following poem written for this occasion.

A year ago today
We walked into this room
    cautiously…
        quietly…
            even suspiciously…
A stray kitten…
    Ready to sprint…
        At my dish of warm milk.
A year ago today,
Bottled and corked
Like chardonnay,
    tears,
        despair,
            exhaustion,
                aloneness,
                    fear,
                        even hatred.
Today, the cat curls himself
Satlated with trust.
His light-footed entrances
Confirm the journey taken
Since that first offering in a dish.
The nature of what he is
Leads him into disappearing acts
Known only to him.
Today, uncorked, we burst and flow
With all that we were a year ago, and more.
Today, a bond stronger than despair,

Aloneness, broken selves.
A bond stronger than that thief
Who had brought us here a year ago.
Happy Anniversary.

May 7

On my cholesterol-free, stomach-flattening walk this afternoon, I thought, "If we (the poets of *Mosaic Moon*) were never to write any poems again, we would still be who we have become. We would not return to who we were as care-givers before we were poets. Our poetic antennae have humanized us with perceptions and understanding of what caregiving is all about. We have found our human souls, and no silencing of our pens could take any of this away from us. Poetry brought us here, but we would not need poetry to keep us here. Now if only poetry could flatten flabby stom-achs and cellulite thighs!"

March 11

This is the second anniversary of our journaling and poetry support group and we are still thriving with new members, as well as some of the original few. The new ones remind me of how the charter members were at our first meeting – the anger, fear, confusion and "why me?" ques-tions. I have this desire to hurry them along the path to where we are, but I know only time can do that along with the support of the group members. They need to walk the same path we did.

So how are the caregivers benefiting from writing poetry and journal entries? Simply put, we became poet-caregivers, a simple act that has made all the difference in our lives. Writing distanced us from some of the ugliness of this disease. And it allowed us to face that ugliness with creativity and beauty through our poetry. Many of us, for example, confronted with the results of incontinence, were already thinking of our pens while cleaning up. The reality of that moment did not strand us there. Instead, we rose to the divine. Here's how two of our group described this phenomenon:

- Sets: "When Frances said the source of writing is myself, and that once I release my poem to others, it no longer belongs to me, I found this to be very helpful in letting go of my negative feelings. Writing releases my burden, and the creative process and the poem form a balanced perspective in the healing and transforming of the burden I carry. This returns me to my caregiving with love, compassion and understanding."

- Lani: "Most important is writing's ability to act as a safety valve for my most intense, even dangerous emotions. When I feel I cannot deal with a situation anymore, I write. As I write, many things happen: I vent my anger, I agonize over my sad lot in life, I dump my frustrations, I accuse and rage against the unjustness of it all, I weep the many tears I can't let my family see, because I know they need me to help them maintain the fantasy of the strong family rallying around its weakest member. I let myself be weak and helpless and out of control because I can never be any of these things in real life. Most importantly, I tell the truth, even if truth is uglier than any monster I could ever imagine. The power of the truth lies in its ability to unmask that which we most fear, and show its real nature. The most sinister evil can be defeated if we know and understand its true nature."

Starting Your Own Poetic Journey

1. Find a special place to go to, a place of solitude where you can reflect and write and "feel like a writer."

2. Read poems by other poets for sheer enjoyment. Be aware of how language is used to create certain images.

3. Focus on ONE feeling, idea, thought or experience you have had and write it out in narrative form as you would in a journal. Write this for yourself, paying no attention to spelling, grammar or punctuation. Get it down on paper. Write what's at your gut level. Write what you need to say, not what you ought to say. If you feel ready to use the poetic form, do so without the journal.

4. Write as many entries as you wish, capturing each of your experiences on paper. It may help to compare your feelings or ideas to something more concrete to get closer to the way you wish to express yourself. For example, if being a caregiver takes you to extreme highs and lows, you might envision yourself on a seesaw and describe that feeling you had as a child playing on one. Or if you feel that life is never on course, how about comparing your life to an errant golf ball:

   Sometimes I feel like a golf ball being sliced into the rough, bouncing into sand traps and rolling into water hazards. The fairway and greens, so inviting but so out of reach. Hey, Tiger Woods, where are you?

   Experiment with language and have fun. Don't forget laughter and humor are good for the soul in the direst of times.

5. Select one of your favorite entries and using as few words as possible, rewrite it in poetic form. Do not think of rhymes. Think of the best language you can find to say what you wish to convey. For example, the golf ball entry can be rewritten as:

Life
Like a golf ball,
I am sliced into the rough,
Bounced into sand traps,
Rolled into water hazards.
Tiger Woods, are you an illusion
Beyond my reach?

Suggested Resources

Fletcher, Ralph, *A Writer's Notebook, Unlocking the Writer Within You*, Avon Books, Inc., New York, NY. 1996.

    (A guide to show you how to keep a writer's notebook with entries that can lead to poems, stories, etc.)

Mock, Jeff, *You Can Write Poetry*, Writers Digest Books, Cincinnati, OH. 1998.

    (For beginners, a simple format – explanations, sample poems, practical exercises)

Moustaki, Nikki, *The Complete Idiot's Guide to Writing Poetry*, Alpha Books, Indianapolis, IN. 2001.

    (A reader-friendly book of tips, exercises, definitions and simplified advice on writing poetry. One haiku poem which appears as an example uses simile, not used in traditional haiku poetry.)

Yasuda, Kenneth, *The Japanese Haiku*, Charles E. Tuttle Co., Rutland, VT & Tokyo, Japan. 1957.

    (For writers interested in the true form of the original haiku written by classical Japanese poets. A "true" haiku does not use similes, metaphors or personification. It captures the essence or the "ah-ness" of that one significant moment just as it is, in 17 (5-7-5) syllables on three lines.)

If, after all this, you still feel the need for a guiding hand to help you get started, I extend my own to you. Write to:

    Frances H. Kakugawa
    c/o Watermark Publishing
    1088 Bishop St., Suite 310
    Honolulu, HI 96813

Remember:

    There is in each of us, a poet crying to be heard.
    Do let the poet out, beginning with one word.

Frances H. Kakugawa

A Poet's Declaration

I am a star
In the Milky Way.
I am the crest
On emerald waves.
I am a dewdrop, crystal clear,
Capturing sunbeams in the morning mist.
I am that dust
On butterfly wings.
I am that song
Of a thousand strings.
I am that teardrop
You have kissed.
I am a poet!
I am! I am!
I am that rage
In the thunderstorm.
I am that image
Of a thousand form.
I am magic on each page.
I am a poet!
I am! I am!

The rain came down heavily all day, drumming steadily on the train's metal roof. Aboard the passenger car was Matsue Takahashi, 19, soon to take the name Kakugawa. It was 1930 on the volcanic Big Island of Hawai'i, at once a primal and lush expanse, its aura enhanced by the smell of vegetation wet with rain. The train was traveling from Onomea, Matsue's home, to Kapoho, a remote village of tin-roofed dwellings, water tanks and outhouses, barefoot children and kerosene lamps.

Tsune Takahashi
(Matsue's mother),
Sadame, Matsue

The marriage had been arranged by a middleman. When Matsue presented herself, her suitor, Sadame Kakugawa, wanted to laugh, for she had covered her head – all but her eyes – with a towel. They met one other time before the wedding in Kapoho, which would be only their third meeting.

After the ceremony, she sat up all night, afraid to go bed with this stranger who was her husband. But Matsue was far from shy. While young and unmarried and working in the sugar cane fields, she had led her co-workers on a sit-down strike to protest their unreasonable bosses. She was intelligent and a maverick, putting what she thought above convention – sometimes to the anger of her husband. She was the first on the dance floor at PTA meetings, sang at parties, bested men at trumps and in salty language, yet was a sympathetic listener and surrogate mother to many. She was an expert seamstress who could recreate a garment from a photograph. She gave of herself to her five children, but did not sacrifice her identity.

Frances Kakugawa, her middle child, speculates that her mother must have had dreams beyond her narrow, confined life in Kapoho. As a child, Frances silently sided with her father, bowing to conformity, wishing for a mother more like those of her friends.

Matsue worked as a seamstress until 1955, when a volcanic eruption covered part of Kapoho with lava. The Kakugawas moved to a three-acre lot in Pāhoa, where they sold navel oranges, tangerines, anthuriums and red ginger flowers grown on their property.

Frances remembers her mother teaching with few words – knowing when to remain silent, or when not to ask questions about a romance or a sensitive issue. When Frances published her first book of poetry in 1970 and had just returned from the autograph party, Matsue knew that her daughter would rather have been in Greenwich Village than cleaning oranges in Pˉahoa – one of that day's chores. She simply sent Frances into the house and cleaned the oranges herself.

When Sadame Kakugawa died from stomach cancer in 1962, Matsue found employment on a vanda orchid farm, where she worked until 1997. Had she not become ill with Alzheimer's disease, she might be working there still. As Matsue was starting her final line of work, Frances was beginning her own career, for she had dreams far beyond Pāhoa. Armed with a bachelor of education degree from the University of Hawai'i, Frances became a teacher, a university instructor, a writer and a published poet.

When Matsue was first diagnosed with Alzheimer's disease, she sat for hours practicing

Frances and Matsue

her signature, filling more than six composition books, for she would have been ashamed if she couldn't sign her checks in public. Eventually, it was a rare day when she could recognize her children, but she still fought for control and dignity till the end. At least one of Matsue's dreams came true – that she would spend her last years with Frances, who had, after all, become just like her.

Poems by Frances H. Kakugawa

I was but a child
When I wrote my first line of poetry
That senselessly rhymed.
It would be my ticket

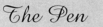
Out of God-forsaken Kapoho:
A ticket away from kerosene lamps,
Outhouses, battery-run radios.
And Pidgin English.
I believed it would be my ticket
To Greenwich Village, New York City,
Paris and Stockholm, Sweden.
Little did I know
That poetry would help me conquer
That debilitating disease, Alzheimer's.
Way before those men and women in white
In laboratory sanctions.

Mother Into Child, Child Into Mother

The same umbilical cord
That had once set me free
Now pulls and tugs me back
To where I had begun.
There must be hidden
Somewhere,
A gift very divine
In this journey back.

Sundown Haiku

She sits quietly
On the third wooden back step.
What thoughts at sundown?

A chill replaces
The warmth of the golden sun.
Will tomorrow come?

Before the thief came
I saw her with all the flaws of an imperfect mother.
I became righteous and judgmental
In my quiet, unspoken perception of her.

Then the thief came quietly into the night
Like that fog on little cat feet
And slowly began to rob her
Of what was rightfully hers since her birth.

Childhood memories,
Dates and places.
Yesterdays and todays,
Even family faces.
Oh so quietly, so silently
Stolen without a sound.

The mother is no longer here,
But a shell of a woman,
Leaving me nothing to judge, nothing at all.
She sits for hours without a past, without a present,
A woman struggling each day to retain
What little dignity the thief had not found
In the tiny remaining crevices of her mind.

My heart aches with love
For the woman she has become.
Perhaps there is a reason for this thief
A final transformation of a mother
Into her purest form,
A newborn babe once again
Before her final journey. ☽

Fall, my second favorite of Earth's seasons
Begins without announcement
Like the first snowflake of winter.
Her photographic display
Matches my wardrobe of earthy tones

Fall

Burnt orange, red, suede, gold, purple, yellow.
In its glory, she moves poets to pens,
Artists to paint, photographers to lenses.
Lovers to love.

Yet, it is a time for dying.
When the rays of the sun
Break into the green of summer leaves
For their final descent.
The final chord of Hallelujah Chorus
Announcing the last breath of life
As all seasons transform into Fall.

It was in the Michigan fall of '62
When a letter from Hawai'i
Sent me straight to my car, camera in my hand.
"Father has cancer and has three months to live."
I drove and drove until I came
To acres of trees crayoned in their glory.
Picture after picture I snapped,
Tears rolling down my cheeks.
Months after the death of my father,
The photos of that day told me clearly
The significance of that day.
In the midst of sadness and sorrow,
I had sought beauty, beauty created
By the last breath of summer.
Today another fall, another season,
Bearing my mother's name.

If I could speak, this is what
My voice would say:

Do not let this thief scare you away.
Do not let this thief intimidate you
Into thinking I am no longer here.

When you see me, tell me quickly
Who you are.
Do not ask me, "Do you know me?"
Help me retain my own dignity
By not forcing me to say,
"No, I don't know who you are."
Save my face by greeting me
With your name even if the thief
Has stolen all that from me.
It shames me to such indignities
To know I do not know you,
Help me in this game of pretension
That this thief has not stolen
Your name from me.

My words have all forsaken me,
My thoughts are all gone.
But do not let this thief
Forsake you from me.
Speak to me for I am still here.
I understand hugs and smiles
And loving kindness.
Speak to me and not around me.
I am not she or her or even a room number.

Emily Dickinson,
I'm Somebody

I am still here.

When I soil my clothing, or do something absurd

Do not tell me, "Why didn't you?"

If I could, I would.

I know I have turned

Into a monstrous baby,

If I could, I would not allow this thief

To let you live and see

What he has stolen from me.

I know my repeated questions

Are like a record player gone bad,

But my words are gone

And this is the only way I know

To make contact with you.

It is my sole way of saying,

Yes, I know you are here.

This thief has stolen

Everything else.

Except for these questions

And soon they, too, will be stolen away.

Yes, I am still here.

Help me keep my dignity.

Help me remain a human being

In this shell of a woman I have become.

I beg that you not violate the person I still am.

In my world of silence.

I am still here.

Oh, I am still here.

Hey Thief.
It's me again. Guess what, Thief.
She's way smarter than you are.
I'll bet you one Social Security check

> That you're sitting there smugly gloating,
> Thinking of all the memories
> You have stolen from her

These past five years.
Wrong, Thief!
You haven't stolen anything.
Every memory that has been hers
Since birth,

> Her trip to Japan at age three
> To say farewell
> To a dying father.

> Her return to Hawai'i
> And being christened Agnes
> By her teacher,
> For the Americanization
> Of the little girl
> Who spoke not a word of English.

> Her work in the cane fields
> As a young single woman
> With still another given name,
> "Strike Boss"
> For leading her co-workers
> To a sit-down strike, to rebel against
> An overly demanding boss.

Her arranged marriage
By her older brother.
It was on her wedding day
That she would see her betrothed
For the third time in her life
As she rode the train
From Onomea to Kapoho
In her splendid bridal kimono
In the downpour of a storm.

Oh, and of how she sat
On the futon on her wedding night,
Unsure of the stranger
Who was now her husband.

All these memories and many more
Have been carefully preserved
In each of her children.
You see, Thief,
She not only fed and clothed
And nurtured her children.
Every significant moment
Of her historical past
Was told again and again
With such storytelling art,
That each memory
Became part of each child.
Did she perhaps suspect
You were already lurking
In her shadows?

So Thief,
Whatever you think you have stolen,
They're still here
Carefully deposited and locked
In each of us who call her Mother,
Only to be released
For the future generations to come.

So I ask you, Thief,
What do you think of that?

Office Visit with Dr. Tanabe

Who is she, this woman
Who speaks so gently to me?
Is she my daughter? She must be.
Only a daughter would speak with such care
And such kindness.
She doesn't call me mother.
She must be someone
Whose face I cannot name.
Did someone call her Doctor?
She asked my permission
To put her stethoscope to my heart.
She thanked me for allowing her to examine me.
Her fingers on my buttons are gentler than mine.
Her hands touch me oh so carefully.
She treats me like I'm crystal and fine china.
So much respect from someone
Whose face I do not know.
Who can she be this most gentle of people
Her voice is so filled with such joy and laughter;
She must be happy to be with me.
But who is she?
I am so confused, is she a daughter
Whose name I've lost?
But she doesn't call me mother.
I can't recall her name or her face.
But this much I know,
This is such a safe place to be.
With someone so gentle and kind.
Who is she?

For Dr. Marianne Tanabe

36

It is 3 a.m.
I am on my hands and knees
With toothbrush in one hand,
A glass of hot tap water in my other,
Scrubbing BM off my mother's
Bathroom floor.

Before a flicker of self pity can set in,
A vivid image enters my mind.
An image of a scarlet feather boa
Impulsively bought from Neiman Marcus,
Delicately wrapped in white tissue
Awaiting in my cedar chest
For some enchanted evening.
The contrast between my illusional lifestyle of feather boas,
Opium perfume and black velvet
And my own reality of toothbrushes,
Bathroom tiles and BM at 3 a.m.
Overwhelms me with silent laughter.

A Feather Boa and a Toothbrush

Yes, yes, yes.
No, no, no.
Yes! No! Yes! No!
The pulling and tugging

<table>
<tr><td></td><td>Leaves nothing</td></tr>
<tr><td>## Tug-of-War</td><td>But bruised palms, sweaty skin,</td></tr>
<tr><td></td><td>Pure exhaustion</td></tr>
</table>

For a game without winners.

The lure is constant
Between caregiver and patient.
The war cannot begin
Unless both ends are held,
One against the other.

Yes, yes, yes,
Yes, yes, yes.
The world held at one end,
No longer exists in the other.
This tug-of-war
Will not bring one into the other
For as long as one end
Is not held for the tugging,
The war cannot begin.

And now for Best Supporting Actress. Me:

for pretending blood in her toilet bowl
doesn't freeze me over.

for being calm with an internal timepiece
that counts to ten when she is found on the floor
after a misstep.

Oscar Time

for pretending her hallucinations of seeing an infant
in bed with her don't scare me half to death.

for nonchalantly cleaning her buttocks, her bedding,
her floor after a bathroom accident.

for wakening her cheerfully every morn with my
singsong, "Good morning, time for breakfast,"
while my body is still lying in bed elsewhere.

for quietly removing a painting from her bedroom
wall after her "Something black is coming out of that
to get me."

for responding to her question as though it is being
asked for the first time instead of a hundred and fifty
times.

for sitting in doctor's and emergency room's lounges
as though it is the chosen place to be, answering to
"Where am I?" every ten seconds.

for never raising my voice although another voice
is screaming inside.

and for saying, "I'm sure you'll live to be 100" instead
of "Dear God, when is this going to end?" ☽

The Center gets smaller and smaller
Slowly squeezing out what once was.

There is no concern of my well-being
As I cough and stumble
Through my own Asian flu.

The Center

How can she be so clueless?
She calls me instead,
"I want to use bathroom!"

Can't you see I'm dying?
I pitifully think,
Can't you see I need caring, too?
Her voice calls again.

There is no interest in the death of a friend,
The birth of a great-grandchild
Or a visit from a son.

The Center is quickly fading
With one last call.
I want… 🌙

Somewhere, someone is listening
To carolers filling the air
With Christmas joy and peace
While the only sounds I hear

Are my mother's voice calling me

A Christmas Memory

And my deep bronchial coughs.

Somewhere, someone is sitting
Near a fireplace, a mug of hot cider in both hands
Surrounded by those she loves
While the only warmth I feel
Comes from my 100° fever,
Compliments of Asian flu, 2000.
My only drink, ginger tea with Echinacea
As I answer my mother's calls.

Somewhere, earth is being purified
By millions of silent snowflakes
Creating Hallmark moments.
The only purification comes
From my bottle of Lysol as I scrub
The bathroom tiles at midnight.

New Year's Eve an encore of Christmas Eve.
My flu has found residence
Permanently, it seems
With that uninvited thief.
At the strike of midnight,
My existence offers no glass slippers
Or carriages into pumpkins.

Determined to be someone outside
Of who I have become,
I pause for Dick Clark
And like everyone else, somewhere,
I greet the New Year,
Singing "Auld Lang Syne."

At the Market:
    Her T-shirt's inside out,
    A label sticks out at her nape
        Displaying not Polo, Liz or Jones N.Y.
        But her size, medium.
        Her mother pushing the cart
        Looks like an ad
        For this month's Vogue.

How to Spot a Caregiver

At the Doctor's Office:
    A well-coiffed mother
    A soft fragrance of Jergens soap
    Pleasantly reveals a recent bath.
    Her caregiver's roots, inches of gray
    A loud cry for L'Oréal
    For she's definitely worth it.
    Or is she running an ad
    For a deodorant?

At the Mall:

> The mother in a wheelchair
> Coordinated picture-perfect
> In a colorful muʻumuʻu,
> Matching vest and shoes.
> Don't look down
> But her caregiver's feet in two different sandals
> Of two different heights.
> But shhhhh, don't tell her,
> She needs her dignity preserved, too.

At End of Day:

> Peacefully she curls
> Into her fetal position,
> A half smile playing on her face.
> The other, a wet dishrag,
> A three-day-old banana peel,
> A marathon runner at the finish line,
> Ready for another sleepless night.
> Good night? ☾

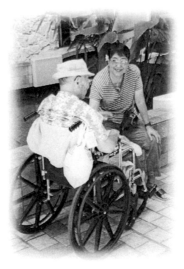

Sometimes

When I'm sitting in the living room,

I'm suddenly filled with unexplainable joy,

Joy that begins from deep within

Joy

And slowly seeks its way toward every pore

Of my body that has become one

With sadness, hopelessness,

Fear and pure exhaustion.

How can this be,

This overwhelming surge of joy

That leaves room for nothing else

When my mother

Is sitting here in the same room,

Silently studying her hands,

Occasionally turning, turning

Her opal ring on her ring finger?

How can I be filled with such pure joy

When the presence of my mother

Reminds me of why we are both here?

What can it be except for

The presence of God,

Whispering, "I am here."

I weep tears of joy

For the two of us.

It was the most exhilarating feeling
When at age 16 I got the key
To the family car and drove solo
All over town through traffic lights

A Thief by Another Name

To country roads and back to home
Where trust was given with license.

Since then, each time I fit that key
Into the ignition and turn it right,
And hear the hum of the engine,
I get to relive that same golden moment
Of 70 years ago.

A moment of complete freedom
As I take complete control of a vehicle,
Freedom to turn right or to left,
Freedom to exceed the speed limit or otherwise.
So many decisions, decisions I am able to make
Because with this key, I am also given
My own dignity! My own capability!
My own manhood! My independence!
With no one telling me
What to do, where to go, how to go.

What exhilaration!
To be the owner of that one key.

The wonder of this freedom
Is one needs to be alone.
One passenger, just one passenger
Takes half of this freedom away.
The AC, speed limit, routes to different places,

They all become half of yours,
When there is but one passenger.
Ah yes, one needs to be alone
Alone behind the wheel.
With a tank full of gas
And nowhere to go.

Today my keys were taken from me. ☾

They both walk toward each other
Each a caregiver from two different condominiums.

A Norman Rockwell Moment

They meet on the sidewalk,
Embraced by the evening breeze
And fragrance of plumeria blossoms.
They both hand each other
A poem written from the most painful
Soul-wrenching depths of
Each of their existence.
They quickly part to return
To tend to the one waiting at home,
For time is not a gift.
Soon each draws comfort
From each other's words
From poems entitled
"Once a Gentle Man" and
"Emily Dickinson, I Am Somebody." ☾

When that day arrives
When I'm not able to spell "world" backwards
Or recall any of the words given to me in a series,
When that day arrives

    When I'm not able to reproduce
    Geometric drawings
    Of triangles overlapping rectangles,
    And not know the day of my birth,

When that day arrives
When the word "Alzheimer's"
Is whispered behind my back,
And Aricept is prescribed,
I'll go out and have some real fun.
Oh yes, I know the secret, you see.
The people all around me will be told,
"It's the illness, it's not her."
Those words will be my ticket to freedom.
Freedom to do all things I've been taught never to do
But always wanted to:

    I will spit in public
    From high places or on sidewalks.
    I will yawn in church, doze
    Or even take a nap.

    "It's the disease," they'll say,
    "Just let her be."

    I'll dress in purple and red,
    Stripes against polka dots.
    Why not socks of different colors,

Spell World Backwards

Red on my left, green on my right.
That'll be okay, wouldn't it
In December near the 25th?

I'll wear tattered underwear.
So what if the paramedics
Don't find Clorox white lacy ones
Should I get hit crossing the street?

I'll dress each finger
With a ring or two
Bracelets on both wrists
That will jangle and clash.

I'll insist on dessert
Before my entrée
Bacon, eggs and rice
For my cholesterol count.

How about my elbow
On the table,
Do a Jack Benny
To rest between bites?

Smoke a cigarette
On a long, slim, silver holder
Like Miss Davis
On silent screen.

No more responses
To every question.
Why I'll just ignore people
At my will.

"It's the disease," they'll say,
"Just let her be."

I'll pick flowers
From my garden
And pass them out
To strangers with sour faces.

I'll send Christmas cards in July,
Gifts for no reason at all.
And smile at strangers
With "Have a great life."

I will have my fun
Until the day
They no longer say,
"Just let her be."

Anxious like a mother with a preschooler,
Hoping for entrance to nursery school,
I sit next to my mother with a silent prayer:
"Please answer all the questions wisely."

Diagnosis: Genius Rejected

"Mrs. Kakugawa", the diagnostician begins,
"What is your name? Where were you born?
How many children do you have?"
Ah, good, good, she's passing with flying colors.

I keep my eyes on his chart,
Checking to see that he marks
The right column, noting Pass.
Positive. Normal.

He upgrades his questioning to:
"Mrs. Kakugawa, you are at Las Vegas airport.
You have lost your airline tickets and it's time to go home.
You have only three dollars. What will you do?"

Without hesitation my mother says,
"I'll put the money back in the slot machine,
Make plenty money and buy another ticket."
"She's a genius," I'm applauding silently.

I watch his pencil move to negative on her chart.
Yes, she should have said, "Use a telephone and like ET,
Call home."
Her ingenuity has no place on this chart.

"Mrs. Kakugawa," he continues.
"You're walking down the street and you find a letter.
It has an address and a stamp on.
Tell me what you'll do with this letter."
Once again my genius in disguise answers,
"I'll check the address and deliver it to the house."
Of course she will. She knows all her neighbors.
Another great step for her brain cells.

Wrong. He marks negative on her chart.
"Increase her Aricept."
I walk my mother out, saddened
That geniuses are off his chart.

"How did I do?" she asks,
"Do I have to pay him? Do I have money?"
"You did super good," I say.
"And no, you don't have to pay him.
He should pay you!"

Rilke's Panther

Like Rilke's Panther
They live behind bars.
There is no pacing.
There is no dance,
For the center
Has been stolen.
They wait for the caged
To be freed from the cage.

Drought

I have become that soil
That slips through the fingers
Of the farmer,
Sucked dry of life.
Will the rains never come?

"Here, take your pick," he offers me.
I look into his Safeway plastic shopping bag
And am greeted with fragrance from pink and yellow plumerias.
"Oh," I say, "Can I have a yellow one? I love yellow."
He smiles and says, "Yes, take your pick."

A Yellow Plumeria

I take a yellow plumeria still wet with dew
And take it to my face to enjoy its fragrance.
He smiles as though he has given me gold.
I gingerly hold the blossom in one hand
As I continue down the aisle with my shopping cart
To find my ginkgo and cranberry capsules.

I turn to look at the man who in one simple instant
Seems to have said, "You are a beautiful woman,
You deserve a flower."

His shirt and oversized pants are wrinkled and caked
Like the rivers that run on his face and down his arms.
His hair, matted with the morning rain, sticks to his neck.
His rubber zoris do not protect his muddy feet.
Yet his eyes shine with pride as he goes from one stranger to the next,
Offering his flowers like Mother Earth each morn.

Soon I see salesclerks with flowers in their hair or behind their ears
And my heart overflows with love for all the strangers
Who have accepted his gift.

The fragrance fills my car as I drive home.
So much fragrance from one simple blossom.
Why am I filled with such joy when all around me
Plumeria trees are in abundance?
Why do I feel so beautiful from one little blossom

Given to me by one flower child,
All grown up in borrowed clothes?
Why do I feel poetic and special all day long?

In late evening I look at the flower, wilted in heat.
If he were my father or my brother,
Would I bless him for his gift
Or would I say, embarrassed, "Stop that. You can't do this.
Don't be a pest. Go home."
Why am I so tolerant toward strangers who give me flowers
But won't allow those close to me to do the same? ☾

Rejoice

out of the cold, unmoving
algae-green waters
of unknown depth
a lotus blossom slowly
raises its face
toward
the
sun.
"I
am
born!" ☾

Anger, it's your turn.
The others have spoken,
Some more eloquently than others,
Compassion, sadness, regret, even guilt.

Today, the podium is yours. Anger.

The Boiling Pot

A wooden puzzle designed for preschoolers
Is placed in front of my 90-year-old mother.
In a singsong voice, appropriate for a toddler,
The program director instructs my mother
To fit the puzzle pieces
Into each empty space.
If only the insertion of the banana
Into the right hollowed-out shape
Could recreate, replenish, impregnate
Cells plagued and tangled in her brain.

I want to scream at their loving efforts
To help stimulate my mother's dying brain
Back to life. I want to snatch the pieces
From my mother's hands and hurl them
Against the wall,
I want to shout, "Stop it! Stop it!"
But I know they can't.
No one can. 🍂

This spirituality of comradeship
Among caregivers
Must make God smile.
Only from His children
> Would such acts of human kindness
> Come forth:

> While keeping vigil
At her dying husband's side,
She looks at me and says,
"When Fred is gone, I'll have time
To help you care for your mother."

Two nights before his funeral,
She brings me cooked pumpkin.
"For your mother," she says.
"This is soft; she will like this."
"This is her favorite," I tell her.

He has been caregiver
For a sister-in-law
All of his married life.
He emails me, "Is there anything I can do?
I am free to go grocery shopping for you."

Her husband is incontinent.
She struggles with his daily changes.
She offers me time and nursing expertise
To help heal my mother's decubitus ulcer.

How God must smile
At all of His children.

He Smiles

Are they the last leaves of Autumn?

John

"You have a beautiful smile."
His eyes, cloudless blue
　　Look into mine
　　Daring me to believe him.

Spring in Autumn

　　I offer him my face.
"Does that come with a kiss?"
For one brief moment
He responds to a flirt.
I feel his kiss on my cheek.

We share a smile.
For that brief moment,
A smile between two strangers,
A man and a woman,
A scene oft repeated in cafés
In Rome, Paris…Elsewhere.

We prolong our smile
Till his caregiver
Comes for him.

Thank you, John.

Are they the last leaves of Autumn,
Aimlessly falling for that last bonfire?

Gambatte, Kakugawa-San

It is her last day at Adult Day Care.
She is held erect by the caregiver.
"This is Mrs. K's last day with us.

She is going to the Health Day Care
Beginning tomorrow."

A moan fills the room.
Do they know the significance
Of this move, that her ability
To walk and to use the bathroom
Has diminished? Will they soon be next?

Spontaneously they sing two Japanese children's songs
And "You are My Sunshine."
Their voices surpass any rehearsed chorale.
One patient quietly stands, walks to a box of Kleenex.
She hands a tissue to my mother
And uses one for her eyes.
Shouts of "Gambatte, Be Strong, Kakugawa–san,
Good-bye"
Fill the room while a few nod in sleep.
I take my mother's hand and lead her out of the room.
Shouts of "Gambatte" follow us
As I search for my own tissue.

The purity of their childlike farewell
Spills over and over
As I drive my mother home.

Mrs. H

She walks out of the bathroom
Just as I am taking my mother in.
Her blouse hanging over her slacks,
She looks at me.
"Is there another way I can wear this blouse?

I notice you always dress nicely.
Can you help me look like you?"

This is her first response to me
In all the months I've seen her.
Alzheimer's had stolen from her, too.

I show her three ways to wear her blouse.
She prefers the first where I tied her blouse
In a knot at her waistband.
She walks back into the bathroom,
Slowly pirouettes before the mirror.
"Yes," she says, "You are smart. I look better."
I nod, one woman to another.

Patrick

We meet for the first time,
McDonald's breakfast before us.
His shy smile and strong handshake
Tell me he knows I am there,
A new face in his home.

He silently eats his eggs and rice
While his caregiver-wife and I chat.
After my second cup of coffee,
He looks straight into my eyes:
"Are you married?"

"No, Patrick, I'm not married.
Nobody wants to marry me.
Don't you think that's terrible?"
He smiles and conceals a chuckle.

His wife adds, "But Patrick, she had many lovers."
He looks at me, smiles and deliberately says,
"Good for you."

After breakfast he is handed his cane
As he slowly tries to find his seat in the living room.
He spreads the morning papers before his face
Leaving us to savor our third cup of coffee.

After our fourth, I take his hand
And bid him goodbye,
"Patrick, it was good to meet you.
I'll come again to see you."

He returns my handshake with a clear, "Good."
I saunter out, sated with womanhood
For all the right things said to me
By this man who still knows
What it is to be a man.

Are they the last leaves of Autumn?
Or is there still a river flowing
Somewhere deep within? ☙

What other path is there
Except the divine?
The other not taken,
Would dishonor not only the woman

Bless the Divine

From whose womb I have come
But also the humanity that is mine.

The Path Not Taken:

Oh, no, how can you be so stupid?
Why are you putting two arms in one sleeve?
Stop playing with your fingers.
Why don't you read or watch the screen?

Can't you feel that noodle hanging down your chin?
You're dropping half your food on your lap.
Don't just sit there, eat.
Use your spoon. Use your spoon.

You're repeating yourself.
Didn't you hear me two minutes ago?
Bathroom again?
But you went just two minutes ago.

Oh, no! You missed the bowl.
Look at the mess!
You just had a bath.
Just look at your dress!

I am so tired, I am so tired.
This is the pits.
What have I done
To deserve this?

When will this end?
Where will it end?
Hear me, somebody.
I'm dying on the vine.

What other path is there
Except the divine
Where love, kindness, compassion,
Help me discover little pieces of myself
That make me smile,
Bringing me such quiet joy
At the end of each day.
When she is gone,
The gift she gave me of myself
Will bring me such sadness
But lasting peace.

It is 3 a.m.
My insomnia-driven thoughts
Wet my pillow.
Somewhere there ought to be
> The lonely call of a train,
> The rhythmic sounds of wheels on tracks
> Diminishing into the night.

But the only sounds I hear
Are boom boxes gunning around
Neighborhood streets.

It is 3 a.m.
There ought to be the cry of a wolf,
Unseen in the moonlit night,
Baying loneliness
To finish my symphony of tears.

3 A.M.

I am a burden,
Whether the sun greets you
From ocean blue skies,
On a picture-perfect morn.

I am a burden,
Whether you gulp in this near perfection
To make it yours,
Forgetting for a moment

I am here.

Dear Caregiver

I am a burden,
Whether dark clouds
Hover over the city,
Forecasting rain
On a Sunday afternoon,
Filling you with an ache
That has no name at all,
I am a burden.

Whether the moon is full or new
In this house that is silenced
By fragmented sleep,
I am a burden.

We live with two thieves, you and I,
And I have become the greater thief
Chiseling away at you
Inch by inch, hour by hour,
Turning you into a kaleidoscope.

Alzheimer's, my nemesis,
No one can yet destroy
But the thief that I have become
Can be expunged.
Free yourself from this thief

With the bond that once existed.
Squeezing out urine from carpets and bedding,
Scrubbing bathroom tiles at 3 a.m.,
Staying up nights, answering his constant calls,
Using your diminishing strength to transport
A thief almost twice your size
Is an act of pure sacrifice,
An act that shatters me like fallen crystal.
It is no longer an act of love,
But one of burden.

We were not joined by blood or vows
For this kind of loving.
The thief has left me with needs
Anyone not bearing your name can meet.
The love that I needed, you have given
Before there was a thief.

We have bade farewell, you and I,
When there was a me.
Let me go before you begin
To crawl in debris of self-destruction.
Set me free in a nursing home
Where the thief I have become
Can no longer be.

To your courage, your love and loyalty
To want to rise above the burden of care,
I press my palms together to you.
But listen to my unspoken words,
It's time to be free.
Free from guilt, sorrow,
Physical and spiritual destruction.
Let us both know peace.
Return us to who we were.

A harpist sends her music
Into our Alzheimer's booth.
I sit entranced, watching
Her fingers run across the strings.

Soon I'm in another world
From where I had come.

A voice jars me back.
He puts his face into mine,
A voice whispered for no one else.
His brows furrowed with fear,
"Do you think I have Alzheimer's?
I often forget what I had gone into a room for?"

Across our booth, a Wheel of Fortune
Offers a free spin for Vegas.
Seniors walk with determination
To join their long line of hopefuls.
A few give our booth a stolen look,
Then quickly turn away.

Music from the harpist
Continues to embrace me.
She does not let the magnified music
Of line dancers stop her fingers.

A man tugs away from his partner
As she tries to pull him to our brochure-covered table.
Have ignorance and avoidance
Become his protective shield against Alzheimer's?

The harpist continues to remind me,

Senior Fair

"If you listen above the noise,
There is beauty in this world."

The bold come directly with their questions,
"Do you think I have Alzheimer's?
I meet my friends and can't recall their names."
The very private begin hypothetically,
"If a person can't remember…
If a person forgets…"
Caregivers stop for confirmation that they are not alone.

A woman dismisses our display
With the sweep of her hands.
"I know everything about Alzheimer's.
My mother is driving me crazy." She walks away.
"No, you don't know everything," I want to shout.
"Look at this with your heart and your soul
And perhaps she won't drive you crazy!"

The harpist continues to soothe me
To a place where peace and serenity exist.
I don't look at my wrist.
"Is it time to return to my mother's side?"
Is momentarily forgotten.

Seniors continue to walk pass our booth
To get in line for free osteoporosis and cholesterol tests.
They climb on shiatsu and massage tables.
They continue to fill their baggies with giveaways,
Ours included.
I can almost hear their thoughts, "Oh no,
Alzheimer's…my own reality…my enemy."

The harpist slowly turns the pages of her book.
Is it on spiritual cue that she stops at "Embraceable You"?
I become one with the harpist, her harp, her music.
My mother awaits; it's time to go.
Her music follows me out, without ending. ☽

A monarch butterfly
Flirts from flower to flower
On a potted zinnia plant,

> Teasing, taunting me, it seems
> Of a freedom I once had.

Wings

> If you had ears,
My delicate little butterfly,
You would hear my voice
Aged with wisdom say,
"Freedom, my dear,
Comes not with wings,
Pretty as they may be.
No, freedom comes
Through the expansion
Of my little mind." ☽

The thief is relentless
In his pursuit:

Ice Cream Cone

"How do I eat this?
What is this?"
Three days ago
There was the crunch of the cone,
Melted vanilla ice cream
Dribbling down her chin,
Caught on her bib.
Three days before the thief came
On little cat feet.

A Pair of Chopsticks, A Rice Bowl

It was her Vegas story to tell,
Asking for chopsticks
In all her dining ventures
In her favorite city of slot machines.
A story to tell
Of a waiter running next door
To fetch her a pair of chopsticks.
"Rice tastes best with chopsticks.
Rice tastes best in a rice bowl."
Meals are now served
In compartmentalized plastic plates
With a spoon.

Often her chipmunk cheeks
Filled with food unswallowed
Reveal another grand theft.

Me

"Where is Hideko?
Are you Hideko?"
Holding my hand tightly,
Fingernails digging into mine,
She searches for me.
Today I am the one being stolen.

The thief is relentless.
He knows, oh how he knows
His pursuit is not yet over.

One thought keeps running through my head
As I sit here holding your hand.

You no longer know my face,
I'm but a stranger who comes to you
As you sit in total silence
Day after day after day.
Whatever thoughts there seem to be
Lay buried deep inside of you.

Somebody's Child

Your brain no longer sends messages
To your colon, to your bladder,
Not even a light whisper.
Your legs no longer know how to walk
Or even crawl. And what I thought
Was so innate with birth, swallowing and chewing
Have disappeared.

Perhaps you are ready to go.
The men in white say you are already gone.
But your heart continues to beat
Deep inside of you where even they cannot see.
Your eyes conceal wherever that you are.
My own limitations do not allow me entry
Inside of you where you exist.

So I sit here holding on tight, for if you go,
I will no longer be Somebody's Child.

Around the dining room table
They sit silently in wheelchairs
Waiting for the dinner cart.

The Equalizer

I look at my mother,
Who rose each morning
Hours before sunrise
To wait on the back steps
For the van to take her
To the flower farm.
Until age 85 she packed
Thousands of vanda orchids a day,
A job she delighted in
Until the day of her diagnosis.

I look at the others gathered around the table
And wonder. Was one a CEO? A farmer?
A surgeon? A clerk ? A dancer?
I want to shout, "What were you?"
It makes not an inch of difference.
They are still men and women
Holding on rightfully to who they are,
Waiting for their plastic trays.

Oh, no, please don't.

"Oh, no, please don't" has become my daily mantra.

How many times do I have to say this

Before I can accept her bizarre behavior

Calmly and with confidence?

Please Don't

Oh, no, why is the salad bowl missing?

Why is it on the dresser in her bedroom?

Oh, no, why is she sitting here

In the living room at 3 a.m.

Insisting "Something is not right."

Oh, no, her words make no sense,

Why is she looking for her mother

Who has been dead for 40 years?

I'm getting nervous and scared.

This fear of losing her

To the Alzheimer's thief

Fills me with uncontrollable fear,

Fear that turns me

Into an incompetent adult,

Wishing somehow I was somewhere else,

Wishing somehow I could walk away, free

Wishing somehow I was a child

And she was my mother as we were before.

Oh, no, please don't.

Four Years Later

The mantra continues…

Oh, no, please don't

Seems like child's play four years ago

A simple plea for help

To stop the course of change
Inflicted by the thief.
A plea based on fear of the unknown
And on one's responsibility to be an adult.
Today the mantra continues
With an ironic twist
Only a mind filled with guilt can wring.

I visit her in her nursing home.
When she greets me by name
Accompanied by a spontaneous smile,
My mantra begins.
When she asks with eyes looking clearly into mine,
"Where am I? Who are all these people?
I need to use the bathroom.
Is it time to go home?"
My mantra begins.

My mantra is silenced
Only when she looks at me blankly
Without recognition,
Calls for herself by name and thinks I'm dead.
My mantra is forgotten
When hallucinations overtake
Her sleeping hours late at night
In images and languages unknown to all.

        Is that the thief's laughter I hear?

When she is alert and seems so aware
Of her surroundings and her life,
And follows Miss Manners in social graces,

A stronger foe obstructs my path:
Guilt.
"Have I made an error in having her here?
Does she belong at home with me instead?"
Oh, no, please don't be so clear of mind,
Oh, no, please don't. 🌙

Mrs. Urata in room 505 died yesterday.
Her daughter's "Frances, my mother just died"
Fills me with sadness.

Mrs. Urata

We had discussed in hallways so many times,
"What a blessing it would be should our mothers
Go quietly into the night."
"Frances, it's very sad when it happens."
Her eyes are tearless, she can't weep, not yet, I know.
Her mother had died just 30 minutes ago.
There are calls to be made.

I lean against the wall in the hallway,
Fighting tears flowing down my face.
I want to sob myself out but I can't, not yet.
Like Lorna, there are things to be done.
Greeting the ladies in the Solarium,
Putting bibs on each, beginning my monologue
As I spoon-feed my mother.

Driving home, I weep for Mrs. Urata.
I didn't know her but my tears won't stop.
When my mother dies and some stranger weeps for her,
What a gift it would be, a gift that will say,
Age and circumstance have nothing to do
With grief.

So often I have heard, "She or he lived a long life,"
Meaning perhaps it's all right for the elderly to die.
Yet, a person at age 90 leaves more memories
Than anyone younger.
A person aged 90 has spent more years
With her loved ones than anyone younger.
Don't we grieve for a 90-year-old for all those memories?

I am still saddened and the tears still flow
For a woman I didn't know.
Perhaps I grieve for her on behalf of my mother
And all the elderly who are still creating memories.

By morning, her name is gone from her door.
I am stunned by such a fast transition,
Then recall how elated I felt
When a bed became available for my own mother.
Somewhere someone is happy and relieved and elated.
Life goes on.
Good-bye, Mrs. Urata. ☾

In memory of Mrs. Shizue Urata

The soldiers stood cemented to the grassy ground
Like statues, while Buddhist sutras filled the air.
Movement would dishonor the man who once stood
In his uniform, like his comrades today.

A Salute to Patrick at Punchbowl Cemetery

The three-gun salute, the wailing taps,
The precision of the folding of the flag,
A salute purified by white gloves
For the presentation of the symbolic flag.

Each step of ultimate precision, a tribute to dignity,
Honor and respect for the fallen soldier,
From the country whom he had served
With love, dignity and honor.

Whatever Alzheimer's had stolen from him,
All was returned to him today.
Whatever memories, forgotten,
The country that he loved, remembered.

A final rest in peace.

"How is your mother?" has turned into "How are you's?"
Where automated responses are given without thought.
Yesterday at the mailboxes,
An acquaintance asked once again,

And the Winner Is...

"How's your mother?"
"My mother?" I said.
"I think she is the prettiest woman
On the entire fifth floor and if they ran a beauty contest
For the elderly, I would enter her and I know she'd win."

She looked at me in discomfort as if to say,
"I wanted you to just say 'Fine.'"

A stranger, slightly younger than my mother
Stood transfixed near his mailbox, eavesdropping.
He waited until I had crowned my mother queen
Before he moved to take the elevator,
A big happy smile on his face and in his eyes,
Hiding his guilt
For lending his ears.
Why did I feel I had made his day? ☾

First Dry Run:

I am a balloon suddenly released from the hands of a child,
Soaring high above concrete streets, man-made walls, rooftops,
Beyond what my eyes can see.

Two Dry Runs on Dying

I am, within minutes, my mother's child
Suddenly transformed into a mature adult,
Capable, responsible, in control of what
I was destined to be.

A desire to shout my revelations, my discovery, my arrival
Silently accompanies me alone to the parking garage.
How can I feel such elation, such freedom, such joy
When minutes ago I had said, " Yes, Doctor,
It's time to let her go.
No more treatments and tests.
If we revive her, it'll be for the nursing home.
What quality of life will that be?
I need to respect her living will and her wishes.
It's time to let her go."

My mother's doctor handing me one of her tissues.
Our eyes meeting without words, a hug, then departure.
All rehearsals done, script memorized.
It is opening night.

I cry myself out in the shower, not for the decision I had made,
Not for the death sentence I had proclaimed,
But for that time that had arrived to honor my mother's living will.
It was a decision easier to come to
Than "Do I take her to ER for her rectal bleeding?
Or shall I wait until Monday morning?
Do I call her doctor about her fever
Or do I give her liquids instead?"

These daily decisions were mine to make,
A responsibility synonymous with caregiving.
Decisions concerning her living will were not mine to make.
I was but a mere voice of her will,
Made years before the thief's invasion.

The next morning my mother revives herself.
I smile and chuckle, "If this was a test,
I had passed with flying colors.
Ah, a mother to the very near end."

Second Dry Run:

Her quiet rambling voice leads me directly to her.
She is lying on her recliner, eyes closed, face peaceful,
Her mouth moving nonstop.

I lean over to hear her words.
Her Japanese is not of her usual vernacular
But of a more formal dialect used with ministers.

She has slipped into her spiritual world.
She is speaking to her dead mother.
"Oh mother, don't you know I'm here?
Of course I'm here. I told you I was coming.
I may have been stupid but I don't think I was bad.
Yes, yes, I have come to be with you."

She soon takes her mother's voice:
"Oh, Matsue, you have come.
I'm so glad you are here.
I told you not to worry, didn't I?
I told you everything would be all right.
There is nothing to worry about, nothing to fear.
I am here."

Her voice then becomes the observer,
Describing a scene of such joy, I, too, feel the joy.
She is being hugged by her mother.
Such joy, so much love.
Matsue is leaping and dancing with joy.

A Buddhist sutra follows.
The entire scenario is repeated
She lifts her hand outward reaching toward someone.
She wants to go somewhere but can't find her way.
I gently nudge her to awaken her.
She opens her eyes, looks at me and shouts with recognition,
"Hideko," then slips into her spiritual world.
Her voice begins again.

Once again I am given a gift.
A gift to let me see how her final transition will be.
She is being loved and comforted in ways no mortal being
Here on earth could ever love her.
She is leaping and dancing with joy,
Joy no place on earth could ever give her.
I, too, am filled with joy
For I know now, my own perceptions
That without my hand in hers, her final journey
Will begin a lonely journey
Is not of my reality, nor hers.
When she dies, she will not need me.
For that final transition, she will have her beloved mother
And her husband, who are waiting for her
With extended arms.
I am but a mortal being. ☾

My house was once so cluttered,
I had no room to move.
No space to step about,
No place to call sweet home.

Clutter

The garbage, waste and residue
Soon stacked against my door,
Locking me in, frozen and chained
Within my own prison walls.

To live or die, to be jailed or free,
Only I could find that key.

My house is now less cluttered,
I've done a lot of cleaning,
Guilt, regrets, falsehoods and despair
No longer fill every space.

Windows are glistening,
Sunlight's peeking through,
Beyond the door, the world awaits
For my return.

The midwife, the first to greet me
In my father's house.
Where he had brought my mother home
Soon after the wedding,

Started the cries that wouldn't stop.
My mother, holding me close
Rocking me throughout the night,

House of Secrets

To hush my cries that violated silence.
It was the mother's plight
To quiet the child at night,
For fathers rose before sunup.
But I held no regards for such lore.
I filled the house with my screams,
Night after night after night,
An infant, confused by night and day,
Womb and Earth, or was I just a brat at birth,
While my mother stayed up nights,
Rocking, rocking, rocking.

At age three I chose the doorway
Between the kitchen and the living room
For my bathroom needs.
I simply refused to be toilet trained,
Like the siblings who preceded me,
Thus the occasional replacement
Of the Japanese *tatami* mat
Disintegrated by my bodily needs.
Beneath the carpet today,
The family secret belonging to me,
Still visible on the wooden floor.

Soon this house of many tales will be sold
So the mother who stayed up at nights
And cleaned the floor I soiled
Will have a place to call home
At Hale Pulama Mau.* 🌙

Nursing facility at Kuakini Medical Center

The maker's gone…
Her web dangles
In the wind,
   As each thread

The Web

   Strangles with dust.

This silken web
Once splendored many,
But that was when
There was a womb.

When I am gone,
Will you say
I was here? 🌙

84

I walk into the flower shop saying,

"I need something for Chinese New Year."

She points to 12 dead branches, raffia bound in a bunch.

"Forsythia," she says, "This is the last bunch.

Hello, Forsythia

Fifteen dollars."

Fifteen dollars for dead branches?

Like a dozen three-year-olds without a nap,

They spread out three to four feet

In every other direction.

They show no sign of any life in any of the branches.

"Forsythia," I say. "How do you spell that?

I've never heard of Forsythia.

Are you sure these are not dead?"

My mother is waiting to be fed; I'm late.

I rush out of the shop with both of my arms

Filled with dead branches, spreading in all directions.

I carefully walk my way through the door.

I can almost hear her, as I leave, "Yes! I got another one!"

I take the dead branches and arrange them in two vases

On my mother's fifth floor. I step aside and look:

At the elevator, against a red backdrop,

A vase sits on an unpainted wooden box,

Filled with dead branches.

They spread out touching the corners, the walls

And space meant for passersby.

They look untouched by human hands,

Undisciplined by the sun, the rain and the wind.

At the nurses' station, another arrangement,

Smaller in size and just as bare.
"Don't throw these out," I warn.
"They're supposed to bloom."

The following day I fall ill and am homebound with fever.
A week later, eager to see my mother, I step into the elevator.
A male clerk greets me with,
"Frances, the branches all bloomed. They are beautiful."
The elevator door closes on his last word.
I step out of the elevator on the fifth floor,
Am stunned into silence.
Every branch and sub-branch
Are covered with yellow flowers,
Against the Chinese red, against the corners, against the wall,
Reaching out toward me into my space.
Forsythia. ☽

Mirror, Mirror, On the Wall

A mirror shattered,
No longer holds my image.
Am I gone forever? ☽

How I feared you,
Cursed you.

The all-powerful, relentless thief, slippery, elusive,
Forever eluding the grasps of Science, a master
Houdini,
Shatterer of dreams, shatterer of lives.
Oh, how I detested you.

Mr. Thief

Today, I bless you.
She lies in bed before her final journey.
She knows no fear, feels no pain, no loneliness
For you have robbed her of these.
She knows only peace as doctors and nurses
Slip silently in and out of her room.
Unaware of her incontinence,
She lives with dignity in her final hours,
With a soft smile playing on her denture-free face.

Moans and screams of pain and confusion
Disrupt the otherwise silent halls of the ward.
No one has stolen their pain
Of cancer-invaded bodies,
Dysfunctional organs and disoriented minds.

Yes, thief, today I bless you.
You have cleansed her of everything
From birth to death, one womb into the other,
A newborn babe shrouded in loving peace.

A fully bloomed gardenia
Sends such fragrance of sensual pleasure
From each unfolded petal.

Gardenia

A woman, concealed in silence
Was once, too, in her own realm
Of such flitting glory.

Dressmaker
Drafting and sewing,
Pumping away at her machine,
Singing songs
Now Japanese oldies,
She dressed the people
Of her village.

Girl Scout
The first Girl Scout Leader
To organize and uniform
The young lasses of her village,
A maverick in her own time
Joining communities
Between unpaved dirt roads.

Dancer
At PTA meetings,
The first on the dance floor
Led by plantation managers.
Active and vivacious,
At *Bon* dances, a dancer,
On Buddhist grounds.

A Surrogate Mother

    A young GI, far from home,

    Nostalgic for his own mother's Italian kitchen,

    Dined on spaghetti sauce and pasta

    In our kitchen of plantation means

    Before being shipped out

    To foreign battlefields after December 7.

Bi-Linguist

    President of her Buddhist Women's Club,

    Giving speeches in Japanese and English,

    The best trump card player

    Among men and women,

    Expletives to match

    Any sailor's tongue.

Therapist

    The confidential therapist

    Lending an ear

    To the young men and women

    Who gathered at her sewing machine.

    A treasure box of intimate love stories

    Never to be shared.

It is not the spotted brown petals of the gardenia
But what it was in its splendor
That will become its final image.

When it is all over
I will shout so all can hear.

"We put up a great fight, didn't we?

We didn't just sit back and cower with fear,
We didn't just sit back and curse this thief
As he quietly stole into our lives.
We knew he was cleverer than us,
His presence so mysteriously elusive
To the men in science. We knew his capture
Would not be in your lifetime
But we didn't sit in quiet desperation, did we?

We knew, didn't we, if I had succumbed
To the burden of care, the thief's laughter would have
Echoed through the walls of our home, and soon,
They would have crumbled.
Had you thrown up your arms in hopelessness
Each time the thief had come, he would have triumphed
Oh, so easily.
But we transcended this thief, you and I.
You held your dignity to the very end.

You walked, sometimes stumbled,
But never did you crawl before this monster thief,
No matter how he distanced you
From who and what you were. Relentless as he was,
He could not rob you of all your memory.
You recalled your childhood and the first family
Who had loved you so, leaving him baffled and dumb.
Every inch of the way, you fought smiling, transcending
Each of the indignities he left in his wake.

*Dylan Thomas,
We Did Not Go
Gentle Into the
Good Night*

90

Had we waited idly in darkened rooms,
For the capture of this thief,
This battle of our human spirit would have been lost.
We called him by name, Alzheimer's,
Thus weakening him with each call.
His Achilles heel we wrapped
With our own pursuit of the Divine.
Whatever he stole, we lived without.

There will be no Nobel Prize for what we did,
Oh, but how we triumphed hour after hour, day after day.
We turned that 36-hour day into a 24-hour day.
We did, didn't we?
With love, dignity, compassion,
Endurance and respect for the human soul,
No match for any prize of any name.
Unattainable by any thief of any size."

When this is over,
Oh, how I will shout in triumph
For the two of us.
Yes! 🌙

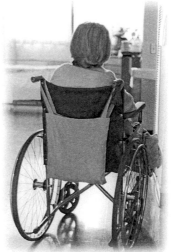

Family Dynamics

Earthquakes of human existence,
Arrive unannounced
First, the gentle trembling under one's feet…
Followed by uncontrollable rocking, crescendoing into
destruction...
Dislodging family heirlooms, soon shattered on floors and
shelves…
Still, the shaking continues like dice in a gambler's hand…
Then stillness once again, among the ruins.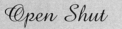

Open Shut

Open shut them, open shut them
Give a little clap.

Silently she opens her mouth
To receive each spoonful,
Like nestlings who open their beaks by instinct.
My voice goes unheeded.
"Three more and you're all finished."
I count aloud with each spoonful of thickened juice,
"One…two…three."
Oops, I miscalculated, there is still another spoonful
In her plastic cup.

I give her the last spoonful and she says, "Four."
The message in her "Four" is clearly heard...
"You don't know how to count
Or are you being condescending to me again?"

Open shut them, open shut them,
Lay them in your lap.

"I brought you some cooked pumpkin,
This is your favorite, remember?
I cooked this for you."
I spoon-feed her, with my broken record
Of, "Isn't this good? This is your favorite."
Halfway through the pumpkin and my broken record,
Her window opens and she says, "Junk!"
"Junk?" I silently say. "Junk? After all the trouble
Of cooking this for you? Such gratitude!"

That evening I serve the rest of the pumpkin
For my dinner, and after one bite, I echo my mother.
"Junk."
Someday I must learn how to select mature pumpkins
At supermarkets. Do I tap them like watermelons
For whatever sounds one listens for?

Open shut them, open shut them,
To your shoulders fly.
Then like little birdies let them
Flutter to the sky.

She has stopped speaking English for a year now,
Reverting back to her childhood Japanese.
A friend of mine visits her,
I introduce him saying, "This is my friend."
She looks at him and says, "How are you?"

"How are you?" I marvel in silence.
How did she know he's haole*?
What happened to her Japanese?

Falling, falling, falling, falling,
Almost to the ground.
Quickly pick them up again
And turn them round and round.

Deafened by the silence
In the dining room
Filled with ladies in wheelchairs
I break out in patriotic songs.
My mother, eyes closed, sings along with me,
"The Battle Hymn of the Republic",
"America, the Beautiful"
And "God Bless America."

Open shut them, open shut them,
Give a little clap…

* *Caucasian*

If you let this thief
Get hold of you,
He'll take you
On a merry-go-round.

The Playground

Round and round you'll go,
Whirling in orbit.
You can't get off
Till the horses all die down.

If you let this thief
Get hold of you,
On to a seesaw he'll lure you,
Up and up and up
Oh so high the breezes kiss,
And as you suck that breath of life
Down you fall to the ground,
Down and down and down.

If you let this thief
Get hold of you,
He'll lure you out to play,
And soon earth's gravity
Will disown you
Upside down and nowhere to go.
While this thief in disguise
Awaits another day.

My question is simple.
How did she know?

For months now, my mother and I
        Have played this same broken tape
        Over and over again:
        "Are you my mother?" she asks.
        "Who are you?"
        Then silence
As I feed her, brush her hair or massage her legs.
Silence.

A Mother's Day Gift

Today, like Rip Van Wrinkle,
Awakened from a deep sleep,
She greets me by name.
"Hideko! Where have you been?
I have been waiting so long for you.
Oh, this is just wonderful that you found me.
Where are you living now? Honolulu?
My, so good you're here."

Later as I feed her by spoonful,
Conversations long forgotten emerge.
"Did you ever get married?
No? Good, good. It's better to be single, you know.
This way, you need to worry only about yourself.
No need to care of a man, humbug!"

"But," I tease her as in healthier days,
"I want to fix you up with a man.
How about a rich, handsome one
Who'll take you to Vegas once a month?"

She bursts into laughter and says,
"No, no, not for me. I don't need a man."
We laugh together,
Two women engaged in silly girl talk.

Our chats transport us to her favorite Las Vegas,
Her work in the orchid vanda fields in Kapoho,
All the places she'd lived since birth.
"This is wonderful you are here.
How very gratifying you found me."

Her eyes are clear, her smile rich with joy.
She acknowledges the blooming pink azalea plant.
She thanks me for all I've done and apologizes
For all the troubles she's caused me.
She smiles and says good-bye when I leave.

What force cleared her plaque-ridden brain
And told her it was Mother's Day?

Next Day: The briefly opened window was sealed.
She knew neither my face nor name.

Somewhere, in the unknown depths
Of her Alzheimer's soul,
Where even geniuses can't see,
There is light.

Why then, would she,

The Lie

Who has quietly eaten her lunch
Without a word and is dozing
In her own private room,
Suddenly look at me and ask,
"Is there enough food for everyone?
Shouldn't we be doing something?
Why are you the only one here?
Shouldn't we be calling everyone?"

Somewhere, in the obvious surface
Of her daughter's mind,
There is a license
To lie.

"Everyone was here," I gently explain.
"Everyone was happy.
You just had a big lunch."

"*Yokatta, Yokatta,*" she says.
"That's good. That's good.
I'm satisfied now.
I'm glad everyone came."

Somewhere, in the mysterious labyrinth
Of her mind,
She knows today is Christmas,
A time for family and food.
We are both comforted

By my lie.

at the very end
as it was
at the beginning
i was the child

she remained the mother

Her Final Breath

she took hold
of time and place

for her final exit
protecting me
child of her womb

the final severance
of the umbilical cord
made easy and gentle
a final gift
from mother to child

the thief once again
failed in his efforts
to switch our roles
for three years she played along
but in her soul, she was always
the mother.

A Thief Worse Than Alzheimer's

Her ashes are still warm.
The path of true grief and love
Returns us to who we truly are.
My sorrow razor sharp,
As my mother slowly becomes one
With the river that holds my name.
Others born of the same womb
Walk in rivers of a stranger name.

From whence did he come
This thief, worse than Alzheimer's,
Who steals human souls,
Emptying the river of God's love?
Wasn't he defeated
In the desert eons ago?

What Do I Know?

Yes, I know,
Her passing is a blessing.
Yes, I know,
There was no quality to her life.
Yes, I know,
She is now at peace.

But when my pillow is wet
At 3 a.m.
And I feel such loneliness
Missing her,
What do I know?

Lynne G. Halevi

Solitude and Loneliness

Loneliness overtakes me,
As I care for my lifelong partner.
Loneliness attacks with a sharp plunge to the
heart.
We were sparring partners.
We engaged in critical analysis of life's occurrences.
His disease has silenced him.
We no longer spar.
We no longer debate critical issues.
Only solitude soothes my mind.
It alone refreshes my soul.
The physicality of caregiving is nothing.
The spiritual and emotional drain,
Complicated by the loneliness,
That is the rub,
That is the pain.
I cherish few moments of solitude.
Only that gives me peace.
Then I can face the loneliness of
A lost love,
A lost companion,
A lost soul.
Loneliness is draining.
Solitude refreshes.

Vic Halevi (at left)

*V*ictor Halevi had his mind made up. When he was 36 years old, he had a serious heart attack and was told he'd never work again. But he would not, as doctors told him to, confine himself to a wheelchair. He simply changed directions.

Born in New York City in 1921 to a Sephardic Jewish family whose ancestry dates back to 11th-Century Spain, Vic was trilingual at an early age, speaking Spanish, French and English. His family moved to Salonika, Greece, to seek out their roots in a vibrant Sephardic community. They moved back to the U.S. after a few years, but when the Nazis destroyed the Jewish community in Salonika during World War II, Vic volunteered for the Army Air Corps. Attaining the rank of captain, he trained navigators (left) and test piloted planes that came back from the war.

Vic wanted to be an actor, so he moved to Los Angeles after the war. In 1948, he met Lynne in a play in which they both acted; seven months later they were married. Lynne says that while Vic was worldly and a bit older (she was 18 to his 27), she had led a sheltered life. He taught her how to drive, swim and do crossword puzzles.

For nine years, they had parts in movies and early TV shows. Their son, Cliff, was born in 1956, and then Vic had his heart attack eight months later. Lynne was told Vic would probably die in two weeks. He ignored the warnings and instead made a bargain with Lynne that they would be together till the end. They moved to northern California where Vic became successful in sales at a major cosmetics company and Lynne went back to school to earn a bachelor's and then a master's degree in speech pathology.

Another heart attack followed in 1970. Again, Vic moved on, this time to Hawai'i. Lynne decided she would work while Vic went to school to become a freshman at age 49. A heart condition wasn't his only difficulty. He was dyslexic and therefore a slow reader, but took up to 30 credits a semester, including a full load during the summer. In three years, he had earned a bachelor's degree in special education and a master's in educational psychology.

In 1975, the couple took their skills to Ajo, Arizona, a rural mining town, where they found satisfaction in helping Native American children with learning disabilities. Another heart incident led to bypass surgery, and then another, but in 1984, he and Lynne took a trip around the world, which ended back in Hawai'i. There they worked with children again, taught at the university, traveled and acted in most of the shows filmed in Hawai'i.

It seemed there was no question Vic would live up to the bargain he had made with Lynne after his first heart attack, but trouble came from an unexpected place. It started with answers that did not correspond to questions asked. Vic had short-term memory loss and was easily agitated. Once a trainer of air navigators, he began to lose his way to familiar places. Lengthy discussions about art and politics became perfunctory, and he refused to do the crossword puzzles they had worked on together daily. Almost all his life he had ignored the odds to succeed, but now Alzheimer's disease was robbing him of his most powerful gift – his mind. But in one way, Vic did not succumb. He had given 50 years of a life that wasn't supposed to be, to live in the heart of a sheltered 18-year-old girl, till the end.

Lynne and Vic

Poems by Lynne G. Halevi

Each tear is a tear in my heart.
If there is a divine spirit,
Please help me to accept this new strange person
Who is disguised as my dear husband.

The River of Tears

I see some vestiges of Vic hidden deep within.
I long for that part of him.
The river of tears keeps flowing.

My Vic, always the careful dresser, now obsessively changes clothes.
The shirts, slacks, underwear and socks stack up on the floor
As he matches each set before he changes clothing.
Constant matching, stacking and changing attire.
The river of tears keeps flowing.

We used to laugh as we said,
"Life for us would end in a giant leap to the other side."
But Vic has broken this bargain.
He is leaving me in a tide pool as he goes in tiny ebbs and flows.
My heart breaks to witness this erosion of the once beautiful beach.
The river of tears keeps flowing.

My eyes water and sting as I hold back the flow.
Down deep the tears and sobs break through the dam.
Outside there are the smiles.
But alone,
The river of tears keeps flowing.

"Damn, damn, damn," I cry.
"Where is the whole person?
It is better to have loved and lost, than never to have loved at all,"
The saying goes.
They don't understand the pain and sorrow

That go with a piecemeal loss.
Tiny fragments of my lost love are almost too hard to bear.
The river of tears keeps flowing.

I yell, I scream, I scold in the pain of loss. He does not understand.
He was my strength, my soul mate and my pillar.
I am abandoned to the Alzheimer's mistress.
He is here beside me in body,
But the sensitive and creative mind is gone.
In his place I find a sometimes stubborn child
Who is not yet toilet trained.
The river of tears keeps flowing.

Help me to have patience and understanding,
While I am cleaning up the spills,
The broken glass, the toileting mistakes.
And observing the obsessive changing of clothing.
The river of tears keeps flowing.

My Vic tries hard to break through the mind fog.
To show me that he is still there loving me.
He sings along with the radio when old love songs play.
He tries to help at dinner by filling and spilling our water glasses,
But forgets to close the refrigerator door, or turn off the water.
The river of tears keeps flowing.

When I cry, he cries and says, "Don't cry," and pats and kisses me.
In bed he clings to me, holds me so I won't disappear into the night.
It is difficult for me to move or turn because of the frantic hold.
I understand.
I love this man/child.
The river of tears keeps flowing.

They want him drugged.
His active brain cells are too much for them.
"He knows how to unlock the gates."

Unwanted in Day Care

They want him drugged.
"He wants to get his own coffee,
We can't have that."

They want him drugged.
I feel slugged.

They want him drugged.
They want to snare the living cells.

They want him drugged.
They want to smash those cells.
They want him drugged.

Oh God, help me find care that is caring.
Care that is loving.
They want him drugged.
I want him.

Bubbie, I'm Not Looking

Sitting at the table, Rachel, age ten, is happily slurping
A rainbow shave ice.
From the kitchen I suddenly hear a frantic,
"Bubbie, I'm not looking!"
I swing around to see Papou, stark naked.
He is carrying his clothing.
Like an innocent child,
He is looking for assistance in dressing.
There is no shame.
There is only one focus,
"Please help me dress."
"Bubbie, I'm not looking!"
Rachel expresses fear at seeing Papou.
She is afraid.
She is unaccustomed to the unexpected.
"Bubbie, I'm not looking!"
Oh dear child,
Please begin to look,
To see,
To feel Papou's bewilderment.
Where he is now childlike,
You must now be mature.
Let me hear you say,
"Bubbie, I'm looking,
Bubbie, I see."

110

Incontinence

What is incontinence?

I picture wet under pants, taken care of with Depends.

Never imagining a volcanic eruption of brown lava

Spewing over bathroom floor, rug, tiles,

And riverlets flowing down legs.

My love is paralyzed with fear.

He gazes at the devastation

That nature has wrought.

I reach for the rags, the wastebasket and the lemon bleach.

Eyes are clouded over, face wet with tears, my nose joining the flow,

I am aware that sobs are coming from some deep cavern.

My love watches sadly, dazedly and weakly.

I mop, scrub and cry.

The brown lava is finally gone.

The rags, disposed in the garbage bag.

How sad to see my once strong partner reduced to this.

He is bewildered as he participates in this unexpected eruption.

While on my knees I say a silent prayer,

"Thank God for my endless supply of rags,

Thank God for disinfectant.

Thank God my love is standing in one spot as I clean him.

Thank God for the strength to cope with this new test.

Thank God for my own eruption of tears and sobs

That cleanse my soul.

Today is my birthday!
A very special day
With ice cream and cake,
Unexpected pleasures.
A day to celebrate.

My Birthday

A day to remember.
Yes, but not this way.
Cleaning brown lumps out of underwear.
Were Depends made for this?

My special day.
A day to remember.
Cleaning his bottom.
Flushing lumps down the toilet.
A day to remember.

My birthday.
My special day.
Now sad.
A day to remember.

A day to celebrate.
"Celebrate what?" I cry?
Oh yes, I celebrate,
Depends,
Baby wipes,
Bleach,
Flushing toilets.

My birthday.
A day to remember.
And yes, a day to give thanks for
Small gifts and big challenges met.
My birthday. 🕊

The care attendant arrives.
I sneak out.
Must keep busy.
Must keep a happy face.

I arrive.
Appointment canceled.
Things are awry.
Must keep busy.
Must keep a happy face.

I drive aimlessly.
Car radio blasts.
Must keep busy.
Must keep a happy face.

Love songs play.
My tears flow.
Must keep busy.
Must keep a happy face.

Love, the wind beneath my sails.
The sails now droop.
The wind dies.
Must keep busy.
Must keep a happy face.

The mind races.
It traces past love.
Must keep busy.
Must keep a happy face.

Must stop thinking.
Must stop weeping.
Must keep busy.
Must keep a happy face.

Keeping Busy

Anger

He is not the same.
I fear the shame of my angry feelings.
His infantile behavior so annoys me.
He pushes, he pulls, he clings.
Sometimes I can't breathe.
I'm angry at this betrayal.
I'm angry at my love.
I'm angry at my loss.
I'm angry at my frustration.
Whatever gods there may be,
Help me to cope with this anger.
Help me to cope with this stranger.
Help me... 🌙

Caregiver's Time Off

Wednesday evening,
Great expectations.
The paid caregiver arrives.
Three hours of total freedom.
I bid farewell amid cries of "No, no, no!"

Freedom, what does that mean?
Three hours without dispensing medicine,
Cleaning messes, washing soiled clothing,
Bathing, feeding, soothing.
Freedom, an unknown factor.

Suddenly released from this totalitarian regime.

I'm lost. How am I to spend this precious freedom?
Do I volunteer at the homeless shelter?

I could make hospital calls.
I could spend time balancing my checkbook.

Do I dare just spend time with no real purpose?
Dare I spend this freedom frivolously?
The choice is mine.
That is freedom's purpose.

I choose to be a spendthrift.
Reaching Borders Books
I move quickly to their second-floor coffee shop.
What a divine view of breaking waves.

The calm of the blue ocean soothes me.
The trade winds clear my cobwebs.
I sit, I look, I watch others.
They drink coffee, talk, read, do research.

They have purpose.
I enjoy my nothingness.
I relish my freedom.
I savor my time off.
A caregiver's freedom has a unique purpose.

The Stress of Lost Love

He is near and yet so far.

I feel his warmth, but not his strength.

I need his strength so badly.

My stress is at times breaking me.

I try to understand, but I fear I'm failing.

I need my best friend.

Where has my love gone?

The spills, the dirty Depends, the laundry.

They all attack my spirit.

They attack me emotionally and physically.

I cry, and I scream a silent scream.

I long to break the silence,

But the scream sticks in my throat.

My love, where has it gone?

Why have I lost it?

I want to find it again.

I want my champion, my strength back.

He is gone.

My love is gone.

Attachment

Attached, tethered, glued,
Magnetized, velcro-ed, siamese-ed.
How many ways can I say,
We are stuck?
I need to breathe.
Where is my space?
I cry for air.
I cry for breath.
I cry for less confinement.
This love is suffocating me.
This love divides me.
My tether is too tight.
I'm gasping for air.
I'm strangling.
I've lost my self.
Loosen my bonds.
Preserve my love.
Detach me.

Guilt, Anger and Remorse

He is gone.

I have remorse.

I have guilt.

I have anger.

Could I have done more?

Why did I shout when he messed his pants?

He could not help it.

I have guilt.

I have remorse.

I loved him so.

Yet I grew angry.

Angry at Alzheimer's for stealing him from me.

Angry at my love for having this disease.

I feel guilt for anger.

I am remorseful for loss.

I loved him so.

He was my bright light,

Now there is darkness.

Hospital Stays

First was the behavior clinic.
That was to adjust medications.
Wrong!
Home again.
Now over-medicated.
Slipping, falling,
Zombie effect.
I'm desperate.
I feel alone.
Call the doctor.
"Don't mess with the medication!"
He is not listening.
People are not hearing me.
I am alone.
Arrive at emergency room.
Tests show Vic is over-medicated.
Second hospital stay is four days.
New doctors are listening.
New doctors are caring.
Family, too, is listening.
Family, too, is caring.
I am no longer alone.

Angels Among Us

Walking alone to the bus,
I met a woman who looked like an Ethiopian Empress.
I was going to the Punahou Carnival.
She had never attended,
Although she has been in Hawai'i since '72.
I invited her to join me.
We had a wonderful time,
Eating fresh hot malasadas,
Viewing the art,
Taste-testing the produce,
And generally people watching.
Mashawn is a nurse and is very spiritual.
I felt a kinship to this beautiful stranger.
I spoke about Vic.
She listened carefully.
I told her that he was in the hospital,
I was to bring him home the next day.
We hugged and parted.
Two nights later.
Vic was home.
Trying to get him to eat when he wouldn't.
Trying to help him to stand when he couldn't.
I was feeling desperate.
The doorbell rang.
Standing there was the Ethiopian Empress
She entered.
She took charge.
She fed him.
Stood him up.

Changed him.
Got him to bed.
I realized then that she is really an angel,
Disguised as a human.
There are angels hidden among us. 🌙

Traveler

We have traveled a long road together.
Now you are a stranger at my side.
Why did Alzheimer's steal you from me?
"How did it happen?" I ask in despair.
We danced, we sang, we played.
Now you cling, you falter, without a song.
The road is bumpy,
Full of potholes.
I hold your hand.
You are lost.
We are companions on this path.
I will lead the way.
You are my travel partner to the end. 🌙

Lani Kaaihue

The Bond

He is the first man I ever loved.
We have pictures of our bond being forged:
A handsome young Hawaiian
Holding a tiny elf, peering out
Under a shock of black hair standing straight up.
We are locked eye to eye.
He's wearing a wry smile
As if thinking, "I'm so lucky
To have someone so precious in my life."
With time, we've changed places.
These days he looks deeply into my eyes to
Communicate through the silence of Alzheimer's.
We lock eye to eye.
I'm wearing the wry smile,
So grateful to be one of his caregivers,
And thinking, "I'm so lucky
To have someone so precious in my life."

*J*oyce Lani Emiko Kaaihue writes of her mother, Winifred: "She still rises at 5:30 a.m. She prepares herself for the day. She tells herself, 'Lani will be here soon; it's six o'clock.' A harsh realization brings pain. She scolds herself, 'No, lady! She's not coming. Dad's not here anymore.' She pours her coffee and sits alone."

Edwin Kaaihue

There was a time not so long ago when a young Winifred Horiuchi was disowned by her parents – until her first child was born – for marrying Edwin Kaaihue. That was in 1950. The problem for Winifred's parents was he wasn't Japanese; he was a pure-blooded, dark-skinned Hawaiian.

Edwin was born in 1925 in Hilo, on the island of Hawai'i. In 1942, he volunteered for the Army. Quickly becoming a staff sergeant, Edwin fought in the Pacific Theater, where he ran through fields with machine gun fire kicking up the dirt between his legs. In 1944, he was highly decorated and honorably discharged.

Returning home, Edwin enrolled in welding school, and later flying school to become a Civil Air Patrol pilot. After they married, he and Winifred moved to Honolulu, where he became a welder at Pearl Harbor Naval Shipyard. In 1952, Edwin suffered from a nearly unbreakable fever. Feeling the illness was job-related, he looked for a new line of work. That year, Lani, the first of four children, was born. She remembers her father as kind and fun-loving, with a good sense of humor.

Edwin worked at the Hawai'i State Prison until retiring in 1978. The prisoners protected him because he was fair, and because he treated them as human beings. Edwin was promoted up the ranks from guard to captain before retiring. But he didn't really retire; he drove tour buses and then worked with golf equipment until 1996, when it came obvious that something was wrong.

Lani always wanted to be a writer, but first she was a Hawaiian studies major, a salesperson and a sales trainer. She worked in restaurants and cabarets, and then went into banking. Starting as a teller, she worked her way up to vice president. Her father had worked too hard, Lani thought, sometimes pulling double shifts for weeks, but now she worked six or seven days a week, and admits her parents hardly saw her.

Winifred and Edwin

Meanwhile, signs of trouble were hovering at the edge of consciousness. Edwin often went to the market for his wife, but by 1994, she had to draw a picture and write what it said on the package she wanted. Then he would come home with something else. Once, he looked at Winifred and for a moment didn't recognize her. By 1996, he couldn't remember his children's names.

Although doctors recommended a nursing home, Winifred refused. Lani describes her mother as weighing 88 pounds but having the will of three. Realizing her mother would soon be the one who was sick, Lani struggled to leave a job she loved, yet now sees it as the best decision of her life. She writes of her former life as "a careless meandering…where the worst stress came from an overflow of meetings and running late in traffic. Such pitiable issues, comparing them now to life and death."

So instead she rose each day to greet her parents at 6:30 a.m., to be at her father's side. Although he could no longer speak or feed himself, Edwin Kaaihue had brought his family together again – with the extreme hardships of caregiving, but sometimes with childish playfulness, or a moment of clarity – until the evening of March 17, 2002, when he drew his last breath.

Poems by Lani Kaaihue

Scanning the faces of my fellow warriors,

I see weariness written across them.

Our troop numbers ten today.

Unlike a military force, we have no unified nation
of citizens to back us.

Siege Warriors

We have no central coordinating body.

Each of us is engaged in guerilla warfare

Against an incorporeal foe.

Our loved ones are under siege by Alzheimer's disease.

Our weapons are Vigilance, Creativity, Curiosity and Patience.

Our health is threatened by exhaustion,

But we must be our own Medics.

Today our General is giving us a tool to heal ourselves – Expression.

A veteran caregiver shares her experience,

Saddening and gladdening us by turns

As she tells of frustration, anger and loss,

Replaced over time by an appreciation of What Is –

Her husband is still with her.

A quiet moment together, sharing a beautiful sunset, home, pets.

The beauty residing in simple things heals her.

Hearing her tale, we are inspired to heal ourselves

United in our determination to defend

And protect those precious others,

We must first be good stewards of our own spirits and bodies.

We labor to loosen the restraints of upbringing,

Inexperience and embarrassment,

Striving to capture intense, elusive feelings,

Binding them in words and phrases

So that, when again this troop of warriors rallies,

We may heal each other and ourselves in the sharing of our stories. ☾

Plateaus

We no longer get too comfortable
Or take a situation for granted.
We've learned that all we have are
Plateaus of unknown duration.
Just as we congratulated ourselves
On having found a day care that
He likes and that is close to home,
He becomes incontinent.
Just as we locate a day care that
Can manage an incontinent participant
And arrange Handi-Van service,
His balance becomes uncertain.
Just as we find the time
To make needed household repairs
Requiring his first overnight respite stay,
He has seizures and cannot walk.
Just as we obtain a wheelchair,
He stabilizes.
We've hit a new plateau and pray that
He can continue to laugh with us.

Aloha, Matsue

Her face glowed, smooth and soft,
Unlined and innocent as a babe's.
Her breaths came slow and even, untroubled.
As we watched over her,
Breathing slowed, then paused.
After several seconds…
Another breath…
A longer pause.
Not an inability to breathe,
Simply a peaceful relaxing.
In these final, intimate moments
She gently left her body behind,
Moving onward to the fullness of forever.

In memory of Matsue Kakugawa

Hard-Working Man

This hard-working man
For whom work is medicine,
Has never been idle while awake.
He worked double shifts regularly
And after work was tired but seldom still,
Since there was always so much to do.
He made and varnished furniture,
Tackled improvement projects large and small,
And kept yard and exterior tidy.
After retirement he found a part-time job
And when his home projects were done
He brought repair jobs home from work.
As cognitive abilities dimmed,
His habits of working hard
Were frustrated by growing confusion.
We locked up his power tools,
Then his cleaning and yard chemicals
And eventually anything that might hurt him.
He paced and paced,
Finding relief in constant motion
Moving plants, newspapers, mail and light furniture.
Now ambulation is limited
But there are new tasks
To keep this hard-working man busy.
Finger Fidgets, Activity Boards and rearranging pillows.
Following silently, we return his arrangements
To starting points so work can continue.
There is a look of fulfillment on his face
Now that he's taught us not to interfere
With work that is medicine.

Torture

We caregivers undergo
Various stages and types of torture,
As brutally atrocious to our spirits
As any inflicted on prisoners-of-war.
Our loved ones are hostages,
Bonded to a twisted Killer
Who mocks the caregiver by
Preserving the familiar face
Of Husband, Wife, Mother or Father,
But trapping their souls in a web
Dangling over a murky abyss.
On good days, you can see that soul
Reaching out to you,
Reminding you so much of yesterdays
That you weep and rejoice in their presence.
On bad days, it is as if some sinister being
That you have never seen before
Resides behind the familiar face,
Like an evil puppetmaster.
The torture is in staying true
To who that person was
Without giving in to believing
That they will ever return.

If you were eavesdropping at the restaurant
You would surely be repelled
By the topic of discussion at our table –
BM!

Speaking of BM…

Six women with cups of coffee,
Muffins, cornbread, pancakes and bacon,
Speak intensely about cleaning up another's
BM!
The stories are told with grimaces and shudders,
Horror that "for better or worse" has come to this
And anger at a situation with no solution –
BM!
The women sigh with resignation.
"I could never" or "I can't" became
"I did" without an alternate choice.
BM!
The experience was not a little thing,
Disgust and frustration lingers.
But the person who was loved is loved still, despite
BM! ☾

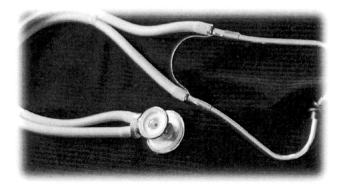

I read about the Lazarus Effect
Not realizing that it would be significant
To me, and to mine.
One day Dad was surefooted but shuffling,

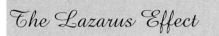
The Lazarus Effect

Patrolling his regular circuit of the yard
Hour after hour, day after day.
The next day Dad was falling.
Hitting his head, blacking an eye,
Breaking two fingers.
We knew his ways
But his abilities changed.
To the ER and doctor we went.
Dad was bruised and bandaged,
But walking on his own again…
The Lazarus Effect.
One day we saw that he struggled
To navigate and balance himself
But walk he did.
The next day spasms shook his leg,
Each recurrence more violent than the last
To the ER and doctor we went.
Medication stopped the seizures
But Dad was groggy and silent,
Unable to rise from his chair.
We lifted him and walked him each day
For a few steps in the family room
As the dosage was slowly reduced.
Dad doesn't remember that balance is tentative
Or that he needs help to rise from his chair,
But he walks again…the Lazarus Effect.

The wheelchair is a reminder
That his abilities will change again
And at some point he will walk no more.
Caregivers pray that the Lazarus Effect is contagious,
So we can bounce back to do what we need to do
Hour after hour, day after day. ☽

Hard heads interfere with good care,
When rejecting those who would dare
To propose changing any routine.

Hard Heads

Why, ideas like that are obscene!
The truth is the issue's too subtle,
For the caregiver's lost in the struggle.
Others try to help the caregiver.
But, believing only she can deliver
The level of care that's deserved,
The caregiver's path will not swerve.
Not allowing herself to be human
She plods on in a daze of exhaustion.
If her heart just believes
She may not have to grieve.
Hope dies hardest in those who're most loving,
She denies the loss that is coming. ☽

In the company of caregivers,
I indulged in memories
Of a loved one slowly fading
From his sense of self and connections,
Into a muffled shadow
Of the genuine person I knew.

In the Company of Caregivers

In the company of caregivers,
I learned that others were fearful
Of the rough word spoken in anger,
Callous responses to repeated questions
And physical manhandling of
Confused, resistant loved ones.

In the company of caregivers,
I spoke openly of the forbidden:
How shame and anger could
Degenerate into denial,
Escalating rare incidents
Into a brutal way of life.

In the company of caregivers,
I confessed frailties and frustrations,
Weakness and desperation,
Countless futile attempts
To solve puzzles without solutions –
Like murders without bodies.

In the company of caregivers
I was accepted with all my failings.
I bonded heart to heart
With other helpers to the helpless,
Gentle defenders of dignity and
Living testaments to love. ☕

The morning crew moves in,
Lighting the bedroom with smiles
And cheery "Good Morning!" greetings.
He lies in bed with hands clutched together,
bright-eyed and aware,
He looks younger than 75.
"How are you?" Mom asks,
And he responds, "Good."
"Oh!" she turns to me, "Maybe he's all better now."
Her words and expression sadden me,
For I see the seductive, destructive traces of Hope there.
I mask my feelings with a smile
As we position ourselves at his head and feet.
Maneuvering his body into a sitting position,
We clean off the urine with a foaming body wash.
He sees himself in the mirror and giggles.
"Hey," he smiles and greets himself.
He carries on a rambling conversation in a language
That is created, then gone, via short-circuiting neurons
That haven't yet taken away his kindly good nature.
We are quite conversant in his non-language
So the three of us have a good time
Exchanging questions, responses and chuckles.
Real world words and phrases are startling surprises
That result in three giggling adults.
We lift him to his feet, holding him steady
Till balance returns.
"I dream sometimes that I'll come in here in the morning,
And he'll be back to his old self," she says.

All Better Now

I say nothing, thinking that my hopes are more humble:
That he can stay at home, surrounded by family, till the end.
She used to say, "I'm afraid to open his door in the morning,
Because I dream that I'll find him dead."
Nothing like human nature to hope…and hope some more,
Till we get to a point where it's all better now. ☙

Disenchantment

My new life beckons.
When can I leave this place
Where every day new sorrows sprout
      To choke the joy out of living?
      A younger, naive version of me
      Once thought that I could remain
Whole, and happy with myself,
Believing family would stand by me.
Now that they have proven to be
Only what they must be,
Disenchantment has broken
My spell of hope and trust.
There is promise in the future
Of a forever loss
That will transform me
Again. ☙

Alone, you began to wander
Through the growing, murky darkness.
Aware and very afraid
Of the dimming of the light.

Together on the Twilight Path

Your words would not align
To capture what you meant.
Time became a slippery rope
That slid through grasping fingers.

Alone, you struggled to conceal
The seriousness of your plight.
So many little signs you gave,
If I had only known.

Alone, I tried to follow
While your aspects fell into shadow.
Aware and very afraid
Of the dimming of the light.

Alone, I struggled to conceal
My frustration with your plight.
I learned too much and too little,
But slowly, enough was revealed.

Alone no more, we've traveled far,
Silent partners in hope and faith.
Keeping every good moment that's left to us,
Together on the Twilight Path.

When a friend's little boy got cancer,
We didn't make it a point to visit.
We could have called our friend
To ask how we might help.

Don't Be Afraid

We didn't, afraid of sadness and sickness.
We cared, but we never let them know.
Now, it's too late.

When a friend's husband got sick
And became housebound with illness,
We wondered how they were faring.
We could have called, but we didn't,
Because we were afraid of interfering.
We cared, but we never let them know.
Now, it's too late.

When my father was diagnosed with Alzheimer's
I worried about mother and his illness.
I asked her to tell me how I could help,
But she always said, "No need."
One day my brother swore at me
And said I wasn't around enough
To understand what was going on.

As usual, I was afraid
To leave the routines of my life and work,
To see the sickness destroying
A man and family I loved.
But I cared, so, I let them know.
Shocked by the excess of need,
I spend a lot of time now
Just being there…No longer afraid.

Drinking the Sea

Being a caregiver
Is like drinking the sea:
Overwhelming magnitude with
No chance of success – Alone.
Yet, with help from others
Even that becomes possible.

The voice calls out, "Where's Hideko?"
Hideko tries not to frown or cry or scold
As she faces her Mother and says,
"I'm Hideko."

Where's Hideko?

In a concerned voice, the day-care attendant says
"She's always asking for someone,
And we can't seem to distract her when she asks,
'Where's Hideko?'"

With a rascally smile accompanied by a sigh
She tells the attendant,
"When she asks, you should go up to her and say,
'I'm Hideko.'"

Walking through a crowded supermarket,
She stops suddenly in an aisle,
Straining to hear what she thought she heard,
A small voice asking, "Where's Hideko?"

"It's just my imagination since I'm so tired
From too many nights with not enough sleep."
Yet she wakes to offer reassurance in the night,
"I'm Hideko."

That children's book, "Where's Waldo?"
Is like her Mother's life now.
There are so many faces in the world, and all seem alike.
Finding a pillar of solidity seems impossible, so she calls out,
"Where's Hideko?"

Without a striped shirt, without glasses or hat, but
Uniquely beautiful, resilient and generous
With talents and blessings,
She brings calmness and peace to Mother
with the simple words,
"I'm Hideko."

In memory of Matsue Kakugawa

I envision the day when he dies
Or the night, if it be so.
I will linger at his bedside,
Holding his hand, if it is free.

Separation

Leaking silent tears,
My body will shudder quietly
Through our separation.

I will engage my family
With all due courtesy,
As if the past held no pain.

After we have celebrated his life
With stories and music,
And solemnly marked his passing
With the flag and rifle salute,
I will leave.
Taking with me only memories
Of his sweet-natured soul
That loved to laugh,
To dance and
To care.

I will live a new life
That will be free of conflicts
With family caregivers
And free of declines in his health.
He will be as free as I will be.
Our separation will be the milestone
Where new paths begin.

That Shiny Sam Brown

The smell of shoe polish
Tells me he's cleaning
That wide shiny belt
I love to see him wear
Over his uniform, with the
Holster and gun at his side.
I take off my school shoes,
Pulling open the screen door
To sneak quietly into the house.
He sits at the kitchen table
Covered now with old newspapers.
A flat can of shoe polish
Has a little rag sticking out of it.
It's from an old pajama top
That three brothers have grown through.
Little cowboys with tiny lassos
Disappear into dark black smudges
In the center of the polishing rag.
Dad's brown hands move smoothly,
Rhythmically up and down
The length of the shiny Sam Brown.
Polishing, polishing, until it gleams
Like a ribbon of satiny black metal.

"Hello, Princess!" he says without turning,
Making me jump and squeal in surprise.

We awaken him, saying that we need to get ready for the day.
The bus will be here at eight o'clock
To take him away to day care.
He stares at himself in the mirror and doesn't answer.

He Knows

He knows.

Time to feed him breakfast.
So, a spoonful at a time, we relate what's approaching
As we raise food slowly to his lips.
His mouth opens, he chews and swallows.
He knows.

Time to shave, wash face, comb hair, brush teeth.
We tell him each time what's coming.
And though he scrunches up his face
And blows like a wild man when the toothbrush goes in,
He knows.

Time to wait for the bus outside.
He slips into a nap as sunlight streams through the garage.
He awakes with a start, and I tell him, "I'm here."
He nods silently, calm once again.
He knows.

Time to give him all the love in our hearts.
He sits relaxed in his wheelchair.
He snores softly in his recliner.
He stares fixedly at my face.
He knows. ☾

If not for Dad, what might I be today?
I might be the Mama-san for a brothel
Called Lani's Lei Stand and Massage Parlour,
Located in the heart of Waikīkī.

The self-promoted madame
Of an establishment that grew
Out of an ill-fated party attended
While a 20-something lamb.
Escorted by a dashing black pimp named Juba
Who was more than willing
To initiate this young, ambitious woman
Into the secrets of selling flesh.

If not for Dad, what might I be today?
I might be the militant local version
Of the Patty Hearst of yesteryear.
Lacking the cash and flash
But intensely devoted to making
The Hawaiian cause the world's cause.
All grown out of a surprise arrest of
A 19-year old idealist,
Impassioned with fury,
Inflamed with righteousness,
Surrounded by activists,
And not knowing enough to say no.

If not for Dad, what might I be today?
An alcoholic attorney or a clinically depressed social worker,
Trying mightily to live up to my idealistic ideas
And being beaten down, day after day
By systems that suck the vitality

And heart out of living, caring human beings
Who want nothing but to help their fellows.
Childhood dreams of helping others
And childish hopes of changing the world were
Enlightened by the real-life experience
Of Dad who worked daily with con artists,
Burnt-out professionals and immature new hires.
If not for Dad...

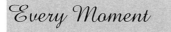

Every Moment

He eats, and I feel comfort.
He laughs, and I feel joy.
He speaks, and the sound of his voice
Frees something inside me
That soars up to the heavens
Proclaiming a bond
That can never be broken.

Every moment together
Is a treasure that I lock
Safely away in memory.
I am a dam bursting,
Unable to contain the fullness
Of my love for him.

Hear Her, Beloved Children

Why is it so hard
To tell those closest to you
How you really feel?
Is it that you're trying to protect
The son and daughter who are grown
Into strong, yet vulnerable adults
From the truth about you?
Why do you struggle alone
To bear the pain and fear
Of sickness that threatens
To devour your earthly body?
Your soul is safe, you know.
Still, it yearns to share this time
With those dear ones
Who are physically close,
Yet spiritually and emotionally
So far, far away.
I hear you calling to them:
Beloved children, now adults,
Please hear the cries of my spirit.
I am lonely and afraid
But I try to be strong for you.
Yet, in doing so, I fear
I am pushing you further away. ☾

Worthy of the efforts of the Bard,
Alzheimer's caregivers inadvertently
Create tragic comedies,
Trying to make sense of

Paradoxes in Caregiving

Paradoxes in caregiving.
The thing that made you happy two days ago –
"Hooray! No BM to clean up!"
Made you anxious yesterday –
"Oh, no! No BM to clean up!"
Its opposite has you positively ecstatic today –
"Oh, thank goodness! A BM to clean up!"
The behavior that made you cringe last year –
"What the heck is he saying and when will he shut up?"
Makes you nostalgic this year –
"I wish he could talk again!"
Your moods work against you
When you least expect them to.
With relief, "Oh, good! It's Monday and he goes off to day care!"
Means "Now I don't have to worry because others will watch him."
Eight hours later you're pacing, awaiting the Handi-Van.
With relief, "Oh, good! He's home from day care!"
Means "Now I don't have to worry because he's back with me!"
Yesterday you said, "If I didn't have to watch him every day,
There are a lot of things I could do."
Today you catch yourself thinking, "I hope he lives a long time yet,
Because if not for him, I don't know what I'd do!" ☾

He treats the elderly, making house calls and visits
To many who move inexorably toward death.
He's clearly touched – the proof is that
The sadness of being old and sick can't abide near him.

Our Doctor, The Madman

He must have been a madman
well before we met him,
Though he looks better than most sane people,
Being tall and well-built,
With sincere blue eyes and
A smile poised to dance across his compassionate demeanor.

One by one, he looks patient and caregiver in the eye,
Shaking hands and greeting us like long lost friends.
A warm smile frames his words, "Hello. How are you?"
Dad has liked him from their first meeting, flashing
A gap-toothed smile that means the feeling runs deep.
Dr. Madman waits patiently,
Giving Dad a pat on the shoulder
Before he asks us, "So, any changes?"
Mother runs through her list of significant events
Marking the progress of the disease.

Listening carefully, he asks questions to focus our memories
And we demonstrate or explain further to clarify.
Dad watches as we talk, trust plain on his face.
Suggestions and more questions from the doctor
Help us to modify our care plan.

I've heard that God shields the innocent and insane.
Dad is returned to innocence, like the littlest babe-in-arms.
Though our good doctor likely lost innocence long ago,

He has surely earned the protection
Of a madly positive outlook
That complements his knowledge, honesty and strength,
Given openly in service to patients and their caregivers.

For Dr. Jon Cooney

Miracle Unfolding

There was a time a few years back
When more than 40 years of loving
Lost all meaning for her.
                    The drudgery of dealing
                    With his most basic functions –
                    Dressing, eating and toileting –
Made her feel less than human.

His vacant stare and
Expressionless face
Made him seem less human, too.
It was partly the medication
She later learned.

But mostly, it was just
The normal progression of
Alzheimer's disease.

A miracle has been unfolding,
Slowly, over the past few months.
He is alert and joyful
When he wakes in the mornings.
His favorite activity is watching her,
His sweetheart, love of his life.
He laughs and talks again
In his garbled, rambling way,
Responding often, with a smile or a nod.

Tucking the blanket around him
One chilly night, she rests her cheek
Lightly on his forehead,
Delighting in his giggle.
"I love you," she tells him,
Surprised to find she means it.
"Do you love me?" she asks,
Not really expecting anything.
He gazes steadily in her eyes
And answers, "Of course!" ☾

No! Dad needs his car!
It's important to a man!
It's his freedom!
My brothers opposed my asking

The Car

To take Dad's car away from him,
Even though he'd already gotten lost
And the doctor said he should stop driving.
My brothers agreed that they'd decide
When Dad was no longer a safe driver.
A brother would be a passenger
On at least a monthly drive
To monitor how Dad was doing.
The moment of truth
Came much sooner
Than any of us had expected.
Luckily no one was dead
And no one got hurt.
Dad was frustrated at first
But soon forgot that he owned a car
After we hid it
One block away in plain sight.

Connecting

I disconnected from family
For nearly 30 years,
Comfortably cocooned in work
That consumed my waking hours
For most days of every week.
Sitting peacefully with my father today,
Not speaking, not looking at each other,
Takes me back to childhood.
He would have an errand to run
And he'd ask if I wanted to come.
We'd sit silently in the car
Enjoying each other's company,
Far away from the babble
Of three brothers and mother.
They were so noisy and loud
That I created a quiet space inside,
To escape their incessant racket.
I could have peace, but was often lonely
When surrounded by them.
I used to wish I could be with Dad
All the time, because he could be quiet
Yet, I never felt lonely with him.
My wish came true after Alzheimer's struck.
Shared, quiet moments are frequent now.
It is, and always was, his Gift –
Connecting to everything important.

A crisis in the family is a heck of a time to learn
About the problems you didn't know about
Between you and the folks you love.
We didn't even know

Family Dynamics

How much pain there was amongst us
Until we spent more time together.
Denial – that a problem even exists
Yelling – as the primary form of communication
Negativity – about the crisis at hand and about each other
Anger – at the world in general, but the nearest
    relative in particular
Manipulation – as a way of dealing with fear
Impulsiveness – using the wrong things to try to get
    to the right place
Control – or the attempt at it, over each other
Sibling Rivalry – long-buried, never-mentioned
    wounds resurface
If any of this sounds familiar,
Welcome to the wonders of Family Dynamics!
At least you should know that it's possible
To survive these very destructive forces.
We did, and because we did,
We are strangely grateful to Alzheimer's disease
For being our common enemy.

Mr. Y came with cash at the ready, asking, "Safe Return?"
Our service club helped the Alzheimer's Association
To register people who might wander from home.
"We'll need a picture of your wife if she's not with you, sir."
        "Oh, no! She's not here! I don't have a picture! I
        can't bring her!
        She can't walk! Why didn't the newspaper article
Say I should bring her!"
The flood of words from this reticent man
Shocked all into silence.
"It's okay," I said, "I'll bring the camera to you."
The next day I went to their house
With tidy landscaping in front.
Inside, a small woman sat still as a sleeping dove on the sofa,
Walker at her side.
He asked her, "Where are your glasses?"
"What? What?" she asked, "Glasses? What?"
"Oh no! Don't tell me you've lost them again!
Where did you put them?
Did you leave them in the bathroom?
Are they still on the dresser?"
He sprinted from the living room
As I carefully closed the front door.
I called out to him, wherever he was,
"It doesn't matter, Mr. Y, we can take the picture anyway!"
She grasped the walker, agitated, and pushed herself up,
Shuffling toward the bedroom where he'd disappeared.
He charged out with glasses in hand.
"Go sit down!" he ordered. "Put on your old glasses!"
Mr. Y told me that his only child, a daughter,

Helped with his wife on Saturdays.
Otherwise he was trapped in the house
With his Alzheimer's demented wife.
Mr. Y had never heard of the Alzheimer's Association
Till he read about Safe Return in the paper.
Mr. Y had never attended a support group meeting.
Mr. Y did not know what to expect
From his slowly worsening wife.
He didn't have time to go to meetings.
He didn't have the Internet or know other caregivers.
He knew that she was his responsibility
So he was doing the best he could.
Mr. Y was very lonely.
Mr. Y was very tired, but Mr. Y could never rest because
His wife would silently leave the house,
Closing the door behind her and shuffling downhill
Till she couldn't walk anymore.
Sometimes she fell. Sometimes she just stopped and cried.
Every time, it broke his heart.

Take Care of Mother

In the middle of a busy workday
I picked up a call, rattling off the customary greeting.
"Lani?" I heard a familiar voice ask.
"Yes, Dad, it's me! So good to hear you!"
"Oh, yes," he said slowly.
"What's up, Dad? Can I do something for you?"
"Well, I think…" Silence.
"Are you okay? Do you need help?"
"Ah, yes…I think…could you…?"
I waited, concerned but not alarmed.
Dad's speech had become more convoluted over time.
It now took careful listening and sleuthing
To make sense of a conversation with him.
"Is it about the veteran's benefits you asked about?"
"Well, yes, and…"
The secretary waved a note at me.
My one o'clock appointment had just arrived.
"And what, Dad?"
"Take care of Mother."
"What did you say, Dad?"
"Take care of Mother."
"I will, Dad, don't worry. Can I call you back later?"
"Uh, okay. Thank you, Lani."
"You're welcome, Dad. Goodbye. Talk with you later!"
"Okay, bye."
I think of that phone call as his last request.
He knew he was ill, and he knew he'd get worse.
All he ever wanted was to take care of his family.

Father lies on his back in bed,
One hand grasping the other.
His eyes are wide and childlike
As he watches us enter his bedroom.
The myriad expressions
That enlivened his face
For the first 69 years of life
Revisit us rarely, on good days.

Raw Canvas

I think of people who donate
Their organs to advance Science.
I wonder if he's made
An agreement with the Almighty
To donate his soul to advance his family.

He's become a raw canvas
On which all of us
Create ourselves anew each day.
Conflicts and history
That formerly pulled us apart
Dissolve in the face of his
Forgetting, forgiving innocence.

Wake-Up Call

It was December,
Just a few weeks before Christmas.
The doctor looked long and hard at me
After hearing my list of difficulties
In the struggle to care for my husband.
He said, "You look tired."

"Of course!" I snapped,
Ready to describe other insults to pride and person endured.
"You should put your husband into a nursing home."
The words were icy hands clutching and squeezing my throat.
I couldn't breathe.
Tears filled my eyes and waves of guilt overwhelmed me,
Had my complaints brought about this sentence of exile?
This was so much worse than the initial diagnosis
Of Alzheimer's disease.
It felt as though I had just lost him,
Again!
He sat quietly in the examining room chair,
Trusting, calmly gazing at nothing
While a storm of emotion raged through me.
Turn over my husband of 49 years to some institution?
Just as he lost the power of speech,
The ability to manage his own bodily functions,
Even the desire to feed himself,
I should turn my back and leave him?
The doctor might as well ask me
To abandon my own helpless infant.
But no, it was different.
Looking back now, I can see that the doctor was right.
I was refusing to accept the consequences of the changes,
And that refusal was slowly killing me.
From the darkest moments of dawn
The glimmerings of awareness.
I searched for a home, and gladly, found none
Satisfying the particular conditions that he requires.
I did find in myself the ability to accept help.
Sometimes the simplest things are the hardest.

Setsuko Yoshida

Can I?

Poems by Frances this morning
Reveal the feeling of the divine
In caregiving.

How can this be?
Can I, too, reach this point
In caring for my 84 year-old husband
Who is returning to childlike ways?

Anger, resentment and frustrations
Overwhelm me at unexpected moments
Throughout the days and nights.

How can I deal with such feelings and thoughts?
Can poetry and journal writing bring me some solace?
To truly see me for who I am?

$\mathcal{H}$e almost never talked about the war, but when Yoshio "Patrick" Yoshida described the prisoners at Dachau, and the fingernails and flesh embedded in the walls, he had tears in his eyes. In a lot of ways, Patrick seemed like a regular guy living in the simpler days of old Hawai'i. Born in 1916, he grew up in a sugar plantation village, played barefoot football, drank beer with friends, fished and played poker on Saturday nights.

He went to the University of Hawai'i under the GI Bill and then blended into the fabric of the community. He married Setsuko "Sets" Tomita in 1950. They spent carefree weekends in rented country houses, went torch fishing at night, and had picnics at beach parks with hot dogs and

*Patrick Yoshida
(at right)*

hamburgers on a *hibachi*. Patrick did what many others did. He became a father (his son Abram was born in 1952). He became a real estate broker and an insurance agent.

However, perfunctory military language on Patrick's discharge papers belie normalcy: "Truck driver, light – Drove a 1/2 ton vehicle (jeep) in combat in European Theater…hauling personnel…" "Operated a tactical field radio…in a field artillery unit in combat…" A soldier in the 442nd Regimental Combat Team, he saw friends die in battle. Talking about feelings and expressing emotion made Patrick uncomfortable, but his experiences shaped him much more deeply than he would let on. Abram feels that after the war, his father's disbelief about what human beings could do to each other was profound, but his experiences gave him the perspective to meet adversity with equanimity and wisdom.

Sets says Patrick weathered hardships with acceptance and serenity. His peace was reflected in the simplicity of a vegetable garden, which became a ritual for him to work. It became a reflection, a culmination of every experience and all he had. "Nothing is as peaceful," he would say. "There is nothing more I want in life."

In 1960, Sets contracted tuberculosis and had subsequent lung surgery. She was hospitalized for one year. Patrick ran the household and cared for nine-year-old Abram alone. He worked full time and visited Sets each night. That same year, he lost his brother in an industrial accident at a sugar mill. Patrick had often spoken of the deep love, respect and loyalty he had for his eldest brother, who worked on a plantation at age 15 to hold a family of seven children together in the absence of an alcoholic father. He would serve his wife twice more in extended illness – in 1992 for a herniated disc and the following year during a major surgery and recovery. It would soon be her turn.

Setsuko and Patrick

Sets had been a registered nurse for 33 years. Working at Hawai'i's largest private hospital, she headed the oncology unit, worked with chronic ventilator patients and devoted much of her career to caring for people with AIDS. In spite of her years of experience, Sets found caring for her own husband a challenge to all she knew as a caregiver, which she expressed in her poetry. Patrick was diagnosed with multifactoral dementia in 1997. The soft-spoken, solidly grounded anchor of her life was giving way not to adversity, but to a disease over which he had no control. He gradually lost cognitive and physical abilities, until he needed help in every activity of daily living.

Although the Patrick she knew has slipped away, his sense of serenity and grounded simplicity still speaks through his garden, and from the inscription on his grave marker, which reads, "Nothing is as peaceful."

Poems by Setsuko Yoshida

Reality

Anger, resentment and frustrations
Explode like an erupting volcano.

Knowing that dementia has robbed my husband
Of his keen memory, his thinking capacity,
Does not help.

Caring for him day after day,
Love, compassion and understanding
Disappear into thin air.

Sitting quietly,
Facing the Buddha altar,
I meditate on my Reality.

My human frailties and limitations
Allow Unhindered Light and Eternal Life
To constantly illuminate and affirm my total being.

With palms together,
I bow in gratitude.

Assumptions and expectations
Of what he can and should do
Must be erased from my mind.
An inner voice reminds me,

> "Be more sensitive and understanding."

His trousers, T-shirt
And long-sleeved flannel shirt
Are placed side by side on top of the bed.
He turns them around and around
Examining them closely.

Not knowing the difference
Between front and back
He wears his T-shirt reversed,
And inside out at times.
When buttoning his flannel shirt,
The buttons are not in alignment
With the buttonholes.

While cooking breakfast,
I look towards the hallway.
He has walked out of the bedroom
Through the hallway to the dining room.

He is standing beside the chair
Wearing his shirt and boxer shorts only,
Thinking he is properly dressed
To sit at the table to eat his meal.

Being Together

He looks like a little boy.
His innocence is so revealing
It warms my heart.
I smile, and tell him
What he has forgotten to wear.
He looks at my face and chuckles
As a glimmer of awareness dawns.

Together, we put on his khaki trousers
Embraced in the centerless circle
Of Boundless Life. 🌙

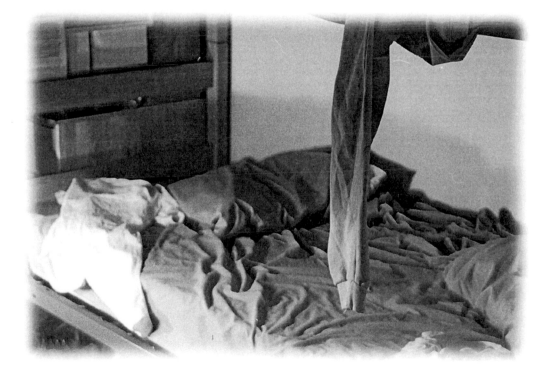

I am awakened abruptly from a deep sleep
At 2:30 a.m.
By the sound of a waterfall.

Night Watch

In the dim night light
I discern the silhouette of a man
Standing and urinating on the carpeted floor
Between two chest of drawers.

I jump out of bed shouting,
"What are you doing?
This is the bedroom
Not the bathroom!"

The blank forlorn look on his face
Sends a message of emptiness.
He does not know where he is,
Nor what is happening
To make me so upset.

I guide him into the shower,
Spray the lower half of his body
With warm water,
Towel dry him and
"Harness" him with Depend,
Not giving him a choice, this time.

I tuck him into bed and
He promptly falls asleep
Like a newborn babe.

Meanwhile, I'm on the floor
With a new roll of Chelsea paper towels
Soaking up the urine
From the carpeted floor.

In the silence of the night
I am struck by
A moment of sadness and helplessness.
"Wow!" there is nothing else for me to do
But clean up this mess!

"With repeated practice
You'll get used to it,"
I hear a caregiver say.

The question for me is
Will I? Will I? Ever?
Be able to accept all this
With serenity
In the midst of my suffering?

The time clock of my mind
Awakens me at 5:30 a.m.
He is sleeping soundly like a child
On top of the bed,

> The lower half in his birthday suit.

> Peeking into the bathroom
> I react in horror!

BM all over the vinyl floor,
Toilet seat and wastebasket!

Inhaling and exhaling deeply
And telling myself
To live in the present moment,
To forget the self,
To single-mindedly immerse myself
To clean up the mess.

Opening wide the jalousie windows
In the bathroom and bedroom
Allows the brisk cool trade winds to dissipate the odor.
No need to spray Lysol Mountain air scent,
I put on the disposable vinyl gloves,
Get a bucket of vinegar water and rags,
Go on my hands and knees
And start cleaning one area at a time.

Emptying my mind of any thought
I follow what Nike says
"Just do it!"

Do It

Four loads of laundry,

Soiled pjs and bvds,

Towels, rugs, sheets, blanket and comforter,

Thankful for Easy Wash stain remover,

Chop Suey Saturday

White vinegar and new lemon Clorox.

Grateful to have a heater for hot running water,

A washer and a dryer, too,

No need to heat buckets of water with firewood

And wash all that soiled laundry with a washboard

Like my childhood days growing up in Hale'iwa.

Being an avid sports fan

I am watching TV

Of the Wimbledon tennis matches

On NBC in the morning

And TNT in the afternoon.

Sampras won, Agassi is winning now

Advancing to the next level

To play stronger opponents tomorrow.

This is my entertainment for the day!

He is resting on his side on top of the bedspread

Stroking Tiger, our striped male cat

Sleeping soundly beside him.

I hear him say in a soft, gentle voice,

"I thank Tiger and I thank you, too,

For taking care of me."

From the potted plants in my backyard
I arrange three orange miniature anthuriums
And ferns, in a short glass vase,
I place them on the Buddha altar.
My mother from the Pureland
Is smiling at me.
I light the candle,
The fragrance of the incense
Permeates the air,
With palms together
I bow in gratitude.

Nature and the simple things of life
Bring quiet joy and contentment
Into my life.

The first days of summer in Hawai'i
Bring longer daylight hours to enjoy:

My husband is lying in the chaise lounge on our patio.
    I am sitting on a cushioned chair beside him
    Under the spreading tangerine tree,
    Surrounded by multicolored bougainvillea
    And beautiful orchid blossoms.

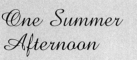

*One Summer
Afternoon*

He is wearing a long-sleeve navy blue flannel shirt,
I am wearing a heavy sweater coat.
We sit quietly with our own thoughts
In complete silence.

Looking out toward the western sky,
Tinged with yellow and orange hues,
The sun will be sinking into the horizon soon.

The cool trade winds caress our faces and feet.
I hear the rustling of leaves of the tangerine tree.
The sound of the loud flapping of the windbreaker
Breaks the silence at intervals.

Being in this rare and precious moment
Brings me inner peace and contentment.
I have nothing more to ask of life.
I am receiving all that I need.

I hear the call of the voiceless voice.
Everything is perfect for me,
Just – as – they – are.

Patrick is gone now,
He has returned home
To his spiritual home of homes
To the land of the Buddhas,

Going Home

A place where his life began
Even before he was born.

I reflect with fond, loving memories
Fifty years of marriage
To a man solidly grounded
Like the rock of Gibraltar.
Sparse words were spoken to express
His deep-felt feelings,
He showed his emotions
Through kind, thoughtful and simple ways.

Experiences shared of joy, pain and sorrow,
Our son and vegetable gardening
Brought him his greatest joy.
We faced many deaths in our family together
Of mothers, fathers, brothers, sisters,
Of nieces, nephews and friends.

As a soldier fighting in the 442nd combat team,
Three years in Europe during the second world war,
He faced his own mortality
Seeing the lives of his buddies being destroyed
By guns, grenades and artillery fire.

The reality of death made him
See the fragility of life,
Appreciating the gift of his unrepeatable life.
He learned to live fully in the present,
Once saying simply,
 "I'm always thinking about life, and
  I'm really satisfied with the way my life is."
Each day was a new day and the last day. ☾

I park my car on the ocean side
Of the temple parking lot.

As I walk up the steps

My Shadow

Of the newly painted
White stairs leading
To the Annex Hall
I stop suddenly
With memories that flood my mind.

"You are beside me, Patrick,
Using your cane
Holding onto my right arm,
I am guiding you to walk
Upstairs, downstairs and
Onto the flat concrete surface.

You struggle to stay upright,
Moving your feet one in front of the other,

Taking small steps ever so slowly
With much difficulty.
Yet, you always make it
To spend the day at the
Hongwanji Respite Center.

I call out your name
And talk to you
But you do not answer.
You live in Nirvana now,
Fully enlightened.

You reach out to comfort me
When I'm alone and feeling lonely,
We are always together
Within Boundless Light and Life
Now and forever more."

It is a warm summer evening,
I am sipping some white wine
Sitting on a makeshift, old wooden chair
Beside the vegetable garden
My husband loves so much.

He is watering the plants,
Drinking beer from a can of Bud
Held in his hand.

Suddenly, he is beside me,
Pointing to a uniquely shaped
Three-dimensional rock
Situated on an elevated mound
Next to the garden.

"Imagine this rock to be
Mt. Everest or Mt. Kilimanjaro,
Human beings struggle so hard
To climb to the top of the mountain,
But, look at the tiny black ants
Who climb up and down this rock mountain
Effortlessly and with ease. That's why
Homo sapiens shouldn't brag so much."

This special rock
Sits on a mound of hardened soil.
Patrick is not with me anymore,
But I hear his voice echoing – "That's why
Homo sapiens shouldn't brag so much." ☽

Conversation with a Rock

Irene Asato

Differences

My point of view was always
Different from mom,
If I said black, she would say white.
Angry and frustrated, I ignored her, calling her old-fashioned.
Our differences separated my love from her.
Then dementia seeped into her life
Making matters even worse.
In denial, I blamed her for everything, not realizing
She was no longer the mom I once knew.
I cried out to the Lord for guidance and strength.
It took years but a change of heart grew inside of me.
Flashbacks of all the grief from the past
Made me realize I was building a wall between us
Based on my fantasy of how life ought to be.
Like the walls of Jericho, my wall crumpled down.
Everything is still not perfect
But she is no longer a burden to me.

*I*rene Naka (Asato) and her brother, David, lived with their mother, Sonoe Naka, in a poor district of Honolulu, in a "Japanese camp." Sonoe was separated from her husband (you didn't divorce in those days, says Irene) with no income from him; he had left in 1948, when Irene was in second grade. He didn't come back into their lives until 1962, when he was seriously burned in an industrial accident. Irene's childhood anger had resolved itself into ambivalence, but Sonoe never expressed resentment.

Irene's mother worked as a housemaid for educated white families and took in laundry. She was interested in her employers' lifestyles and looked up to them, for she felt strongly about education. Sonoe had completed only up to

*Sonoe Naka and
Irene Asato*

sixth grade because her mother died when she was 12, leaving her to become a surrogate parent for a family of four. Well-to-do people would give Sonoe gifts of second-hand clothes, termite-eaten furniture ("It's still good," she would say) and knick-knacks. Although material possessions didn't impress her, Sonoe stacked the gifts all over the family's small bungalow to sell for extra money. Whatever the circumstance, Sonoe would say, "Everything is perfect."

However, all was far from perfect in Irene's eyes. She could not understand her "difficult" and independent mother. Her mother's mind, Irene felt, was on a course as unalterable as a railroad track. She saw her mother as narrow-minded, strong, but without feeling. Sonoe didn't show much physical affection. But at special times like Easter, she would boil eggs the night before and arrange them in baskets. She would go to work early so she could come home in the afternoon to be with her children for the occasion.

On Christmas Day, there would be many presents for Irene and David – a single hairpin in a box, a can of tuna or Spam, a toothbrush – collected since October and carefully wrapped in recycled wrapping paper. Irene didn't appreciate what she saw as quantity over quality, but her mother's joy, she later came to realize, was in giving. It was how she expressed her love.

One day while walking with a friend, Irene saw her mother picking a doll out of the trash.

"It's for a friend's daughter," said Sonoe. "They are so poor."

"But it's embarrassing," Irene protested.

"Embarrassing is when you steal," said her mother plainly.

When Irene was in high school, many of the families of Japanese ancestry left, having the advantage of fathers who saved enough to move. Other people moved in, fragmenting the community, and the sense of safety was

Irene and Sonoe

gone. Eventually the Naka family was able to move out too, thanks to Sonoe's brother, with whom they went to live until a home could be bought.

As soon as she graduated from high school and acquired secretarial skills at business school, Irene move to San Francisco to get away. Later she returned to Hawai'i, in spite of unresolved issues with her mother.

At Christmastime, Irene's two young children would receive numerous presents from their grandmother – a hairpin, a can of tuna, a toothbrush. "They didn't care that the gifts were small," Irene recalled. Somehow, she realized, her children understood her mother in a way she could not.

By 1996, Sonoe was diagnosed with Alzheimer's disease. Irene understood through her children, and now through poetry, that Sonoe's sole mission had been to be a mother. "What would I be without her?" Irene now asks.

"I love you," she tells her mother. "I love you too," Sonoe responds, unconcerned with her daughter's struggle. She says with conviction, "Everything is perfect."

Poems by Irene Asato

My Mother's Visit

When she visited me that morning
She did not stay very long.
Only long enough to see how I was recuperating,
And to deliver her homemade bouquet of plumerias
In a jelly jar she used as a vase.
Her three oranges and apples in a paper bag
Were her fruit basket. After she left,
My tears ran down my cheeks.
All I could think of was her kind face, warm well wishes,
Her caring heart.
I knew she had walked a distance,
Caught the bus to come to the hospital,
Never imposing on anyone to take her place,
Very independent, self-sufficient,
Not wanting to bother anyone.
I looked around my room filled with beautiful bouquets
Of many spring flowers, sunflowers, roses galore
And elaborate fruit baskets.
My mom's gifts stood out and my heart burst with joy.
How blessed I am.
I knew God had mended my relationship with my mom.

My mom is a plain and simple woman
Who always wore the same dress style,
Her hair rolled up in a bun,
Never wearing any makeup.

But she had a kind and beautiful smile
That just made me feel good.

Simple and Effective

She never finished school –
Only to the sixth grade,
But she had wisdom
That she instilled in my brother and me.

She struggled as a single parent and at times
I am sure, she questioned, "Oh, what's the use?"
But she never complained or showed it to us.
Instead she persevered – never turning back.

"Nothing in life comes for free," she would say,
"You must work hard for anything you want.
Be good citizens, for God is watching you."
She was just proud of us being ourselves and said,
"Be the best in whatever you do."

A Thorn in My Flesh

Suddenly I'm in the midst of it...
Words I've never dreamed of,
Alzheimer, dementia, senility,
An illness that is so heartbreaking.
Not accepting my mom's illness
And being in total denial
Runs me ragged.
It was like paddling upstream
In a torrent current
Draining whatever energy left in me,
A losing battle.
Exhausting at times, I cry myself to sleep.

A new day arises and my mom, totally oblivious
To what is happening
Starts her day all over again.
"Love conquers all," the Bible quotes.
How can you love someone unlovable or mean?

Acceptance – knowing she has an illness
Becomes a breakthrough for me.
It isn't easy but at the end of the day,
Knowing I did the best I could
Gives me inner peace and forgiveness
To conquer another day.
Hugging her and loving her becomes a healing process
For the both of us. ☾

Support Group

A caregiver's haven
Where stories told,
Tell me I'm not alone.
Peace overcomes me…
Letting my guard down…
Sharing from my heart
My deepest wounds…
Accusations of stealing…
Hallucinations…
Hiding things…
Not recognizing your loved ones,
Are but a few… but stories everyone
Relates to and is willing to share from the heart,
Makes me feel I am not alone.

My mom, once headstrong, independent, feisty,
A one-track mind, not an easy person to deal with,
But now, frail, body hunched, hardly able to walk
And sometimes difficult to take around.

Saimin* for Lunch

But there is joy, the joy I get in watching her.
Her favorite lunch is saimin* and Coca Cola.
She picks up the saimin with her chopsticks,
Noodles falling on her dress
But she eats them so patiently,
Not getting frustrated, chewing every bit,
Lifting up the bowl to her lips to sip the broth.
I point to the red-and-white fishcake,
Ask her if she knows what it is.
"*Kamaboko,*" she says.
That surprises me. She remembers!
What a sight to see her, tears in my eyes,
My normal reaction would be of embarrassment
Of the mess she created.
But, instead I have a sense of joy in my heart.
Gratitude fills me to be blessed
With a change of heart,
Not getting impatient, but
Having the love,
Compassion and empathy for her,
Thanking God for the opportunity
To serve her with a willing heart.
She is not a burden anymore,
But a child of God, innocent, helpless and loving.

* *Japanese noodles*

187

Here it is Sunday, an afternoon planned for my mom.
A thought of taking her to the park,
Spurred for that moment.
Why not, it turned out to be a beautiful day.
I hurriedly go to pick her up at the care home.

At the Park

She is quietly eating her lunch
With her roommates.
I sit on the sofa looking at her, waiting.
Does she recognize me?
She looks at me as if I'm a stranger.
Doesn't she know I'm waiting for her?
I drive her to the park and in spite of the crowd,
A couple drives off, a parking space meant for us.
We walk toward the ocean, an empty picnic table.
I quickly rush over to reserve it.
The hustle and bustle of the surrounding area
Echoes in our ears.
The aroma of meat charcoaling on the grill,
Children laughing, running and jumping,
The sun warming us with the cool trade winds.
Baskets of food are unloaded on the picnic tables
Surrounded by colorful balloons blowing in the air.
A sign, "Melissa's Birthday Party," displayed prominently
Where others can see.

I take out a banana, peel it and hand it to my mom
Who seems to enjoy it.
Next I peel an orange and pass it to her,
One segment at a time.
The last of the entrées – a package of crème crackers.
A feast for a perfect afternoon.

Mom

Your body is slowing down with age,
Toes crippled with arthritis,
Your memory is slowly disappearing.
But yet, whenever I see and ask you,
"How are you doing?"
You always reply, "Everything is perfect."

Jody Mishan

Sacred Time

You gentle spirit. You strong hero.
Your fine, soft white hair
Creating a halo around your innocent face.
You break into a smile and it makes my day.
You lie in bed, tucked in and content,
And I feel blessed that you are safe.
Who would have known that the love
I feel for you now, as I care for you daily,
Would so far transcend the typical love
Of a daughter for her father?
How else would I have ever really understood
What compassion is?
Or what it is to be a hero.
You break my heart and you make it whole again.
The disease you endure with such bravery and grace
Will not let go of you.
All I can do is protect you from discomfort,
Unfairness, pain, loneliness.
I can wrap you in a cocoon of normalcy,
Fill your days with little expressions of love.
How long a journey will this be
Before you slip away from me forever?
I don't want you to suffer,
So I sacrifice my days to share them with you.
Now. When you need me there so much.
Together, we are God's children. And this time is sacred.

*T*here's a scrapbook of old photos of a muscular, very handsome, 18-year-old man, John Edward Mishan, who studied forestry at Syracuse University, then joined the Navy in 1942. During World War II, he flew small scout seaplanes over North Africa on secret missions. One of the photos shows John Mishan receiving the Distinguished Flying Cross for valor (left).

John Mishan (at right)

There are pictures, too, of a pretty nurse, Maria, who worked in New York City, these pictures above an inked caption reading "My Sweetheart." John once flew a plane under the George Washington Bridge to impress her. The couple was married in 1944, and there are glamorous photos of them in nightclubs in New York, New Orleans and other places. John had tours of duty all over the world, teaching aviation in London, at the University of California at Berkeley and elsewhere. He was also stationed in Hawai'i, Midway Island, Washington State, Rhode Island, California, at the Pentagon and in Japan.

John and Maria had two daughters, Jody and Marlena. Jody Mishan became a writer and producer and also works for an organization with the vision to improve end-of-life care in Hawai'i. She studied drama and was accepted to the Yale Drama School's MFA acting program. However, she was also once a rebellious teenager, who often terrified her parents by staying out till 4 a.m. when they lived in New York City.

When John received orders to Guam as chief of staff, the move took Jody away from the city's "bad influences." She was angry with her father, but in retrospect grateful for his tough but gentle love. Jody's mother opened a successful gift boutique in Guam. After retiring in 1973 with the rank of captain, John returned to Guam, helped get funding for a new airport and sold real estate.

Jody says her father was a hard worker and a respected officer. He was self-disciplined, never drank too much or smoked. Although frugal, he tried his best to accommodate the three extravagant women in his life. He was always there when they needed him. He enjoyed swimming, too. He would swim laps in deep ocean, then come back to bask in the sun for hours. Jody believes he enjoyed these times the most.

In 1989, Jody's mother was diagnosed with cancer. As she lay near death, she said softly to Jody, "Poor Daddy." When she died, Jody saw her father cry for the first time and, as she held him, noticed how vulnerable he had become.

Nine years later, John, who had since moved to Florida, visited Jody in Honolulu. But now her father, who knew numbers well enough to do his own taxes, couldn't remember how to write checks. He no longer initiated trips to the beach. He trailed behind as the two walked together, and substituted strange words for common ones.

"Daddy, you can't live alone anymore," Jody said with concern. She saw tears well up in his eyes for the second time in her life. He said, "I think you're right." Six months later, John stopped making sense; he was diagnosed with

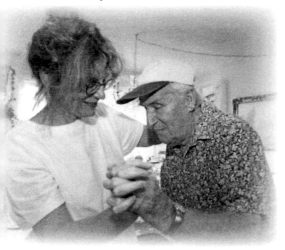

Jody and John

Alzheimer's disease. Jody brought him to her home in Hawai'i. In spite of the dementia, John remains gentlemanly and kind, appreciative of his caregivers.

There are new photos now – of Jody and her father walking hand-in-hand in a park and dancing in the living room – but it is clear that the once muscular and very handsome man no longer leads. Jody still sees a hero in her father, braving each loss of a basic skill. She reflects on how they have become closer than ever, only for him to slip away.

Not long ago, when Jody reminded her father that he is still a hero, he looked at her and said intently, "*You're* a hero, and should be honored for it."

Poems by Jody Mishan

Precious man. Father. Hero.
You gave me so much, so many times.
Now I give back to you, and try to grow up
Without your guidance anymore.

Hero

Only your example.
You depend on me for everything now,
As I depended on you.

I learn patience, courage, compassion, unconditional love.
I fought for you, saved you – and you repay me
With your smiles and contentment.
I find such beauty in your aged face,
Your little eyes, still so blue.
Your set expression, showing how all the thoughts
You used to have
Have emptied out, leaving only sensation.
It is a look of bewilderment, or a look of nothingness,
Or a look of worry.
I want to wipe the lines off your face.
I want to find out what makes you happy now.
But you are an enigma, buried in this illness.
I do my best, as you did your best.
I must be satisfied
By the presence of all these angels.

Layer by layer my identity
Imperceptibly falls away
Until one day I wake up
And no longer know what I want,
Who I am.

Pearl

I pad myself with more food, more weight
To feel nurtured at least.
I shove responsibilities to myself and others
Under the rug.
An old familiar voice inside me says,
"I want to be free."
But the new voice says,
"Later. Right now you must care for Dad.
You are now in a monastery
Devoted to a Higher Cause.
You are now getting a Ph.D. in Alzheimer's Caregiving."
Which voice do I listen to?
Which one is the right one?
I shove the conflict under the rug as well,
Just to get through the day.
The days that I get through
Have turned into months, a year...
I try and find myself from time to time,
With differing levels of passion.
I give up, then try again.

I nourish my spirit when I can,
And find the strength to go on.
But I want out.
I want to be free of the prison.
I want to graduate.
But then a spontaneous exchange of love
Warms my heart and soul,
Showing me again
That this prison sentence is a gateway
To understanding compassion.
That compassion is stronger than fear or anger.
I am thankful again.
Grace wins. Love works.
So I go on. And on. And on.

Lost

I had a dream last night
That I lost my mother and father at the same
time.
I awoke with tears, realizing I had been sobbing
Into someone's arms.

I realized I was awake and OK.
As reality seeped in, I relaxed.
It was only a dream.

My mother did die, but 11 years ago.
My father is asleep down the hall now,
Half lost to me from Alzheimer's disease.

But knowing he is still around
Comforted me immensely.
Even though it's not him anymore,
It is a warm body, loving heart and gracious soul.

This made me realize
I did not want to lose him yet,
Even though he himself is lost.

When did it go?

It visits so rarely, or not at all.

Will it ever return?

Buried under layers and layers of flab:

> A fatty mental substance

> Invading the brains of Alzheimer's caregivers.

> No matter how hard you try

To keep up the appearance of normalcy and control

Of remembering details as before

Of getting something totally right, perfect...

Something always happens to show you ungracefully

That you can't think straight anymore.

You leave the house with only half of what you need.

Did you leave your brain in the refrigerator?

You forget to wear your watch.

You didn't bring the directions, the cell phone, the mail.

Forget to put on your ring you usually wear daily.

You put the milk in the freezer.

> Is it that you can't wait to get away

> > And rush to escape the caregiver and your significantly
> > "Other?"

> > > Desperately seeking precious free time?

> > > > Or is it that you're trying too hard

> > > > > To gather all the pieces of your own fragmented life?

> > > > > > And you have only several hours to do it.

A relay race
Before the next watch,
The next dinner planned,
The next long vigil,
The next chunk of hours,
Catering to you-know-who.
Monotonous routine supervision and coaching
Of your Alzheimer's-stricken loved one.
Your husband or wife, mother or father.

Details about them usurp your thinking process.
Doctors, appointments, groceries, toileting, policing,
Are they warm or cool enough,
Whoops, didn't lock the door, give them their pill.
They have grown like seeds of a banyan,
Like a smothering vine, carpeting your healthy branches.
Looking nice to the outside passersby.
But inside, oxygen-deprived.

Details usurp your clarity
Like a covert operation you're not aware of
Until it's too late.
You can't even detect now when it started.
Quickly and prolifically
The flab accumulates,

Obliterating your ability to reason.
Another day of less than perfect.
You can't find it when you need it anymore.
You make heroic efforts to take baby steps of
Managed and strategized daily work plans.

No matter how hard you try
Things that used to be easy and effortless
Take all your time and concentration.
You can't solve the simplest problems.
Another dose of stress knocks down your
Fragile house of toothpicks.

You can't plan.
You don't finish things.
Your head is full of noise
That no one else hears.
You're too vigilant to meditate.
Will you ever be able to think straight again?
You have faith you will.
But for now, you give up trying.
It feels too much like being retarded.
It's too scary to think it's contagious.
That you've become stupid. ☾

Grotto

If you could peek inside the caregiver,
Peel off the layer upon layer
Of exhaustion, scattered thoughts,
Any combination of ambivalent emotions,
You would be drawn into
A museum of artifacts.
You would want to linger more,
Drawn to artworks so subtle
And universal in relevance
That you would want to study them.
The caregiver's soul is an art form.
A marriage of craft and talent,
The result of which
Is tenderness, compassion, honor,
Vigilance, strength, courage.
An ocean of commitment.
A true heart.
A romantic spirit.

It is the profoundest beauty
That makes art.
That is the rock in the mine.

For so long not noticed,
Your attention casts a light
That would reveal
Glistening crystal clusters
Grown in the dark.
Now bathed in light, casting rainbows
In all directions.

So many tender moments pass us
When I pour love out to Daddy
So unconditionally and hugely
That it slowly caused him to glow.

He is now my creation.
Before I was his.

I speak the limited language he still understands.
I learn his basic vocabulary.
He still knows the familiar.
He says one day, "I like you very much."
On another morning he enthusiastically asks,
"I'd like you to marry me."
I laugh and tell him I'm his daughter.
I point to the photograph of mother in his room.
"See Daddy? That's mother, your wife –
You were married, remember?"
He says nothing, hoping to get by
With yet another non-response
To mask his total lack of comprehension.

I like it best when my love for him
Is not poisoned by the horrible behaviors.
When love wins out,
When patience replaces anger.
When he pees in his pants, or all over the rug,
I try hard to see him as a helpless child
Desperately in need of dignity,
A man whose feelings can still be hurt.
I feel so sorry for him,
Knowing the grave losses he has suffered
And has yet to endure.
He seems so unaware of them,
Not depressed, just smiling a lot.

The caregiver and I
Smile and laugh with him frequently.
He makes us laugh.
Our laughing seems to lull him
Into a belief that everything is good.
He's in a bubble of comfort
That I pay for at a very high price:
My own freedom.
The hourly wage to the caregiver.
My independence and free time.
My regular exercising at the times I would like.
Meditating without interruption.
Going out at night.

So much has been suspended
To accommodate his illness.
I pretend that life is somewhat normal,
When it's far from that.
But when I see him content and relaxed
I feel suddenly deeply gratified
That I have taken all these moments in time
And filled them with love and support for him.

Downplaying his disabilities.
Helping him do so many things every day:
Eating, toileting, washing his face and hands.
Adjusting his pillows and blankets.
Moving his legs and shoulders in bed
So he doesn't lie diagonally with his feet dangling.
All the necessary comforts
That make him feel secure.

I am sometimes filled with such peace and joy
Knowing that what we share
Is God's Presence. ☙

In anticipation of his shower,

Daddy says, "So, we'll have a cleanliness massage."

One day, first thing in the morning

When he walks into my room, he states,

"I love you and want to get married."

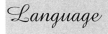

Language

I say, "But I'm your daughter – we can't get married!"

He replies, "OK,

I'll respect your wisdom in these matters."

Another day after he wanders away

And I have to call the police who bring him home

Two hours later…

I am shampooing his hair in the shower,

Rubbing his head, telling him he should never do that again.

And he quips, "Don't rub it in," smiling ear to ear.

Once I tell him he's a handsome man, and he says,

"Maybe 30 years ago. Maybe 100 years ago."

The caregiver tells him he has nice hair, and he replies,

"What little there is left of it."

One day I remind him that he had won

The Distinguished Flying Cross in WWII, and that he's a hero.

He looks me in the eye, driving the point home and says to me:

"*You're* a hero, and should be honored for it."

My head throbs with stress,
Aches from dealing with this mess.
I hate tonight.
One of the sinister menagerie of emotions
     Spawned by Alzheimer's disease.

Stress

    It eats away at our hearts.
    It sucks the marrow of our strength.
Our immune system and adrenaline
Goes into overdrive and malfunctions.
Coping with crisis after crisis.
Mess after mess.
It takes its toll.

Anger tonight.
I rage at Hawai'i.
A state that's still in the Dark Ages,
In not having progressive, accessible or affordable
Alzheimer's facilities.
I rage at my father
Who had not the foresight that this might happen.
For leaving me with
Dysfunctional remnants of our family,

This disease has destroyed
The fragile little family we did have.
Turning siblings into enemies.
It is only me who is left to be responsible for him,
Because no one else will sacrifice.

I rage that life was stripped of all its splendor,
One appendage at a time.
Each dissection left me with a few functioning parts,
So it didn't seem so bad.
But now there's hardly anything left.
And I'm exhausted, uninspired, too numb
To renew my spirit.
Just needing rest.

I finally look back and see all the wrong turns,
And that I can't turn back.
It's too late.
But going forward seems barren, short, unexciting.
Not worth pursuing the future anymore,
Not with this heavy burden.

Is the caregiving killing me?
This fear is always there.
I beg God to help me through these dark times.
To give me strength.
If I did not have prayer at times like this
I could not have made it this far. 🐦

Moonbeams

We are the moonbeams.
The caregivers who support each other.
We are the circle of wounded spirits
That come together to sing our hearts out.
We take back the night and bloom together in the dark.
We are flowers of the night, sweet and true.
Through writing and sharing
We reawaken the sleeping spirit
And celebrate our beauty.

I realized today that my days are largely spent
Dealing with my father and the toilet,
My father and three meals a day.
So, the time I have to endure

Waste and Time

Tediously expelling liquid waste
From my *own* body
At inconvenient but predictable times,
And waiting with great boredom and impatience
For the turds to fall…
Wondering why I did not bring a book or crossword puzzle…
This time is now compounded
With having to not only wait so there is no accident,
But to help take his pants down and pull them back up,
Wipe him, clean his bathroom, wash his hands.
So you take the times I have to go
And multiply it times two each day.
Then there are the meals.
Thinking ahead hours to make sure he is fed.
What will be on the menu tonight?
No, no time to meditate or go running.
I must prepare the meal,
So he can eat, go to the bathroom and sleep
All over again, day after day.

I remember a time as a teenager,
That time when nothing can touch you,
When you can conquer the world,
When you have so many dreams and promises
Waiting around the bend.
When men look at you with lust.

When you have power, but no brains.
I remember my philosophy
Of hating going to the bathroom, sleeping and eating.
I found these activities boring, a waste of time.
I pondered how much more
We could get done in life without them
Taking up all our time.
What amazing, creative feats we could accomplish,
If we didn't have to be bothered to empty our bladders,
Or stuff our faces, or lose hours in unconsciousness.
I rebelled against our human mediocrity.

So how ironic that in middle age
I must perform these mediocre tasks,
Not only for myself,
But for someone else, over and over again.
Saying "Good for you, Daddy" when I hear the tinkle.
Feeling relieved that at least for now
I don't have to clean it off the floor,
Or wash his wet pants,
Or deodorize the rug.
"Good man!" He aimed right this time.
Or, saying "Wonderful, Dad!
Good for you! That was a big doo doo!"
And feeling elated as I wipe his butt,
Knowing that we can now go out in the car
Without worrying about making a pit stop
Somewhere inconvenient.
This is my life?

Where is that teenager who challenged mediocrity?
That preferred dreams to reality,
That refused to participate in anything
Less than perfection, pleasure, art, cutting-edge fashion,
Love, sex, music, travel, passion – Life!

If you take all these moments in the bathroom,
Buying, preparing, serving food,
Cleaning up from both…
Multiply them all by two…
How many hours a day are spent
On what goes in or out the holes.
I wonder…
Could I win the Nobel Peace Prize, an Oscar or Pulitzer
If I could use that time for more creative endeavors?

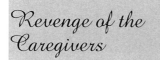

Revenge of the Caregivers

Alzheimer's disease.
I name you and defy you.
You are a witch
That shapes people into animals,
Loved ones into strangers,
Time into a Thief.
But your spell can be broken
With each act of love,
Each commitment to care.
I have conquered you many times.
Your days are numbered.

"Come here. Come here. C'mon.
That's good, that's a good man!"
I coax him everywhere he needs to go;
Otherwise, he'd end up in the wrong place.

My Pet Father

"Time to get out now, Dad…
Get out of the car! Open up the door.
Out. Out! Get out."
A litany, as I carry the groceries in.
He sits there, perplexed,
Perfectly satisfied to remain in the front seat.
I open the door for him and carry some more bags in,
Feeling like a pack mule.
Five minutes later, he's still there, frozen.
Again, "Out of the car, Dad!"
He moves a bit.
"That's right…get out. C'mon.
Get out of the car.
Get. Out. Of. The. Car.
C'mon. Put your legs out."
I'm training a dog who doesn't learn.
But I have learned to be patient.

My litanies and appeals are repeated
Each day, hourly, predictably.
So I recite them like lines in a play,
Varied in subtle ways with each performance,
Much like whistling or humming.
"It's cute," I think to myself.
"He's cute, like a little child.
Like a pet. A pet Daddy."
A high-maintenance pet Poppa doll.

I can comb his hair,
Wash his eyes,
Kiss and hug him when he looks adorable.

I've trained him to smile with love,
Dance a few steps upon occasion,
Reach out for my hand to lead him on our way.
Behaving with relative contentment,
As long as the routine is maintained,
Meals are served at the same times, showers are given,
Bed is made comfortable.
Vets will tell you that dogs thrive in this environment.

If I had known
That seeing my father as a pet
Would become a coping mechanism
In my fiftieth year,
Could I have prepared myself?
No, I don't think so.
No one could dream of a future like this.
It doesn't match that perfect picture
Of the kind and respected older gentleman,
Sharing stories and dinners,
Swimming laps in the ocean with you
On sunny holidays at the beach,
Saying, "You can't beat weather like this!…
You couldn't have a better day
Anywhere in the world!…
The water's cold, but it's refreshing after you get used to it."

The water's cold, but it's refreshing after you get used to it.
It is and I have. 🍂

Nerds Anonymous

Are we caregivers all nerds?
Totally absorbed in one thing,
Isolated from the world,
No social life.
Wearing uncool, ummatched clothing,
Repressed, self-conscious,
Able to relax only in the company
Of other caregivers.
Part of a system
That doesn't understand, help or support us.
Geeks. Nerds. Caregivers.
No dates on Satuday nights.
Not really party people.
Our humor is not normal anymore.
Hello. My name is Jody.
I'm a caregiver and I'm a nerd,
And I no longer have control of my life.

Thriving

Our care recipients are plants
Needing sunlight, water and love.
In order to thrive
We fuss, we clip, we weed, we water.

I've had to put him on different windowsills
Hoping he would catch the light.

Doctor not communicative. Change doctor.
Medicine makes him worse. Stop giving it.
Nurse's aide insensitive. Don't have her here again.
Day care makes him act out. Try another one.
That one sits him at a craft table all day.
Keep him home.

Every day is the right mix of water, light and food.
You are rewarded with blossoms of their joy and peace.
Sprouts of lucidity.
Finding the right routine
Can be a challenge.

And then, as if it wasn't already difficult
There will come a time
That in order for them to thrive
We must let them go. 🌙

It's beginning to sink in.

Who I've become,

Because of you.

Caregiving has hatched an egg.

Inside, a lovable tiny bird.

A fuzzy little symbol of hope.

Kept warm with love and patience.

Now I can celebrate and be joyful

For the person I've become

By caring for you.

Your last big gift to me…

Teaching me to love myself too,

Be proud.

The love we share,

Altered by your Alzheimer's disease,

Is all the more precious and rare.

Thank you for that joy

Of being in my skin.

For the rest of my life knowing

I gave you the best care I could.

My beauty is deep.

My spirit will fly. ☙

Wings of Love

In Memoriam

Patrick Yoshio Yoshida
January 6, 1916 - October 26, 2000

Victor I. Halevi
April 25, 1921 - March 17, 2001

Lillian Toshie Kimura
July 27, 1923 - August 1, 2001

Matsue Kakugawa
February 4, 1911 - January 16, 2002

Edwin Kaaihue
June 18, 1925 - March 17, 2002